PRAISE FOR
UNPACK YOUR EXISTENCE

I enjoy reading every page of this book. I am enjoying aha! and yes! experiences as I take part in what is being communicated. As if something dormant in me has awakened. The content is a wonderful mix of, among other things, classical psychology, cognitive behavioral therapy, Byron Katie's The Work and a lot of psychosynthesis.

What psychosynthesis has in common with Unpack Your Existence is several psychological models of how we humans can function. The most interesting, in my opinion, is that we are also part of something bigger. And that life is magical. These authors convey this in a concrete and clear way without frills. There are good exercises that are easy to absorb and inspire me as a therapist. With subtle humor and seriousness, appropriate quotes and sayings are delivered in each chapter. It becomes an extra spice that makes me sometimes smile, even laugh at myself. This book makes me happy, and I will put it in the hands of anyone who wants to learn more about themselves.

Kerstin Brezina,
Dipl. Psychosynthesis Therapist

This book contains the wisdom of the ages distilled to produce a masterpiece of information. Overall the breadth and scope of the text is amazing. Congratulations on this work of art. It is a legacy that will be visited by many and utilized to create greater happiness in the world. It is a honor to know you. I am implementing some of these concepts already and this was a gift to get me going.

Dr. Steve Ruden,
co-creator of the Havening Techniques

UNPACK YOUR EXISTENCE

UNPACK YOUR EXISTENCE

A HYPNOTIC EXPLORATION

DON T. BIDOUX
FREDRIK PRAESTO
ULF SANDSTRÖM

Published by the Institute of Behaviour Design

Disclaimer

The authors of this book does not dispense medical advice or prescribe the use of any technique as a form of treatment for physical, emotional, or medical problems without the advice of a physician, either directly or indirectly. The intent of the authors is only to offer information of a general nature to help you in your quest for emotional well-being. In the event you use any of the information in this book for yourself or others, the authors assume no responsibility for your actions.

978-91-987382-4-7 (Paperback)
978-91-987382-1-6 (Hardback – Collector's Edition)
978-91-987382-5-4 (eBook)
978-91-987382-3-0 (Audiobook)

Editing: Nina Shoroplova, ninashoroplova.ca
Publishing Consulting: Geoff Affleck, AuthorPreneur Publishing Inc., geoffaffleck.com
Cover artwork by: Zizi Iryaspraha Subiyarta, Pagatana.com
Typesetting: Amit Dey, amitdey2528@gmail.com
Illustrations are from: Briefe Über Alexander von Humboldt's Kosmos, 1850
Illustrations on pages 133 & 175 by Anna Pers Bräcke
Art on page i and page 234 by Alice Sandström

There is a reason
why you are reading this book

INTRODUCTION

This is the kind of book that may confuse you. You can put it down, go back, pick it up, read some more, and smile. Hopefully. It is designed to open minds and hearts, and each has different needs and speeds.

You are one of the notes in the symphony of the universe as it unfolds this very moment. You are a dance between the physical boundaries of your body and your limitless soul, observed by your consciousness in the acoustics of your environment.

Your thoughts and emotions are your guides between adventure and survival as you navigate toward pleasure, meaning, connection, yearning, and love.

Imagine falling asleep and dreaming that you wake up lost in a strange landscape, finding a treasure map and beginning to follow it, now ...

Don T. Bidoux, Fredrik Praesto, Ulf Sandström

FOREWORD
BY JUDITH SIMON PRAGER

It has been my life's work to teach a unique form of communication for healing and emotional wellbeing around the world. So, when I was asked to write the foreword to this book written by people I so admire, I gladly accepted.

Little did I know, when I began to read it, that it was a depth probe into the farthest reaches of ideas we may be capable of traveling, and at warp speed. I suspect you'll jump in and find yourself taking a deep dive among tableaux that will grab your ankle or catch your eye. You'll stare fixedly in wonder and then come up for air to absorb the experience before diving in again into yet another timeless space.

You'll be swimming in metaphors, floating in fantasies, amidst the gem-filled universe of these pages. Grab each jewel, come out into the light, bring it with you to be dazzled by its many facets. And then feel the energetic pull of it all, back into the next terrain.

I suppose it's been the wonder of it all that has stimulated my metaphorical words.

The joy of the authors—their insights, their enthusiasm, their clear excitement about how much bigger, wiser, and more magical we can be—is contagious. Your mind is invited to welcome in every astonishing idea, every challenge to the You that you thought you knew, every limit you ever unconsciously set for yourself.

This is a magical book. As scientists pursue the Theory of Everything to connect all the physical aspects of the Universe, the dynamic ideas here might be viewed as the Lived Experience of the Theory of Everything.

Unpack Your Existence lets you test run the ideas through a prism of every aspect of your being. As Don T. Bidoux, Fredrik Praesto, and Ulf Sandström say, "Your mind wants to understand; your body wants to survive and thrive; your genes want to adapt and replicate; and your soul wants to evolve, connect, and express itself. When these dimensions are in tune and aligned you can choose what songs to play."

You always knew there was more, you just didn't know how to wrap your own YOU around it so that whatever isn't you, the old programs and all those supposed and believed limits melt away.

Captains of whale-watching boats have told me that when swimmers encounter pods of dolphins, they come up exhilarated. Being in this sea of wonder created by these authors is like being in the presence of dolphins. Take this dive. You will be enriched, and you will emerge exhilarated and free.

Judith Simon Prager, PhD,
author of *Verbal First Aid* and *The Worst Is Over*

FOREWORD
BY JOHN LA VALLE

I have read many, many books on "self-development" and have found little in the way they're written that would genuinely help another person to help themselves. Too many want to appeal to us—through jargon and big words—with what we don't know about ourselves.

As a matter of learning strategy execution, one of the essential elements that move people to the success of their choosing is whether or not they can "experience" change in the "real" sense of the word. So, I have warnings for you about this book!

DO NOT BE FOOLED by its stated simplicity. DO NOT BE FOOLED by the white space. DO NOT BE FOOLED about the easily understandable words.

This book is fully loaded with such simplicity that its effects on human development can be very pervasive within the reality of how you can experience your own experience. And this is how personal change is done: by experiencing your own experiences and making your own decisions based on those experiences, rather than accept what anyone else can determine without being you who has the experience.

As you read through these pages, enjoy the depth of the impact that it has on you. Think about how easily your changes happen and don't be surprised as much as you will because I warned you from the start about its simplicity.

John La Valle,
Master Trainer of NLP and
co-author of *Persuasion Engineering*®

Transformation starts in exploring the doable.

~ Don T. Bidoux

CONTENTS

Contents

Alice was beginning to get very tired of sitting by her sister on the bank, and of having nothing to do: once or twice she had peeped into the book her sister was reading, but it had no pictures or conversations in it, "and what is the use of a book," thought Alice "without pictures or conversations?"

~ Lewis Carroll, in *Alice's Adventures in Wonderland*

YOU ARE THE CREATOR

All people are similar, and everyone is different. You are a dynamic flow of amazing and continuous adaptation to life. Now is the time to do this on purpose. Enjoy the ride.

Creating the Creator,
your symphony is
enough already.

CREATE THE CREATOR

*It's all in your head, you just have no idea
how big your head is.*

~ Lon Milo DuQuette

The adventure of life includes exploring and unleashing the potential of the specific time and circumstances you live in.

Your most powerful companion is your imagination. It is the source of every human action, piece of art, improvement, and discovery. It can motivate you to boldly go where no man has gone before and it can allow you to spend a wonderful night at home with a smile. It is the voice in your head that creates the images and notions that guide you. Choose words that paint a map you wish to explore.

The very nature of your imagination is to be limitless in ways the physical world isn't.

On the one hand you have an amazing potential stored in the wizardry of your genes, a self-regenerating body, an environment with oxygen to breathe, and gravitation to keep you from drifting into space. On the other hand, you have an imagination that can invent ways to breathe underwater and fly you to the moon.

Among the most wonderful, and potentially dangerous, abilities of human imagination is the ability to unite and collaborate around an idea. To facilitate communication over thousands of years we have invented writing, and to spread it instantly around the world we have built the mighty internet. It isn't norms and laws that rule society, it is how we imagine them ruling us. You are as free as you imagine yourself to be. We are as united as we think we are. Let's make sure we pick the right ideas to collaborate around.

Stress is created by your imagination, but so is calm. Standing between you and your potential are your ideas of what is possible. Allow these ideas to evolve, and so will your plans and actions.

You can use your imagination to transform your experiences, memories, beliefs, and emotional responses into strategies and knowledge, into the kind of wisdom that allows you to truly explore the full experience of life.

Essence

" *Imagination offers you an ocean of possibilities. Get wet.* **"**

Explore the Physiology of Your Beliefs

1. Focus on a belief about something that seems to limit you.

2. Ask yourself: "What if it is so?"

3. Ask yourself: "What if it isn't so?"

4. Shift your physiology, body position, movement, breathing.

5. Think of somebody else—real or imagined—who would believe differently.

6. Imagine what they would do.

7. Imagine doing it.

A seed remains just so until planted.

~ Don T. Bidoux

YOUR SYMPHONY

*No person ever steps in the same river twice, for it's
not the same river and it's not the same person.*

~ Heraclitus, Greek philosopher

Life is a river of moments that you flow through, and you
are what you think, feel, and do in each of these moments.

There is no consensus as to what a personality truly consists
of, to what degree it is genetically predisposed, how much
it is shaped from life experiences and how much it can be
changed. Historically, our personality traits have been
described from a static perspective of usefulness or disorder.
Now is the time for this to change.

Your personality is like the flow of a symphony. The physical instrument of your body and its musical DNA sounds so
much better in tune. A musician who is fed, rested, and cared
for performs better.

The acoustics of the concert hall and the sounds made by the
other instruments are a constantly changing environment

that sends signals to your senses to be acted upon, consciously or not. Where the river flows.

The audience adds a different dimension, changes the energy, the tension, the magic. The harmony, rhythm, and dynamics are what you think, what you feel, and what you do. The intended melody of the composer meets reality guided by the director who leads your orchestra, looking to bring out your best in any given moment. Your soul.

The resulting symphony is a map beyond what can be described by pure science, psychology, experience-based observations and beliefs. Some characteristics of the orchestra are inherent and some are intuitively self-learned or intentionally trained. Some of your thoughts, feelings, and behaviors are what make you unique in your taste of art, thoughts about the meaning of life, and how you choose to dance.

Your body is where you are; your mind is where you find it; and your soul is you beyond survival and daily maintenance. The result of all of this is an action of some form; it is what you "do."

Essence

> *The symphony of you evolves through the instruments, the acoustics, the audience, and the way the music is directed.*

Explore Your Symphony

1. If you were an instrument, which type of instrument is that instrument?
2. What can you do to be in tune, and ready?
3. If you can choose a new director, who would it be?
4. Who is writing the notes?
5. What is the tempo?
6. How are the acoustics of your current concert hall?
7. What happens if the audience shifts?

What matters, in the end, is the relationships we build, the people we love, and the meals we share.

~ Brazilian proverb

ENOUGH ALREADY

You can change or stay the same, there are no rules
to this thing. We can make the best or the worst of it.
I hope you make the best of it.

~ Eric Roth

Imagine a person who has potential beyond what they may be aware of. A person who deserves your respect; the main character in a plot unfolding before you.

A lot of people create their beliefs early on about who they are and hold onto this identity dearly because it provides a sense of predictability and certainty for everybody involved. However, neuroscience has shown that your brain has an amazing plasticity that allows you to learn new things and change as long as you live. This includes your beliefs about yourself.

Your self-esteem is a collection of beliefs about your value, and is in many ways more fiction than fact. If you do your best you will always be good enough, and stating anything else is defying gravity. You were born being enough, and your life is a process of finding out how much more *enoughness* you can develop along the way. This is why it is best to compare your progress with your earlier self and use the enoughness of others for inspiration.

The past you, the future you, and the present you are the same team, Team You. Be the support you need. Find the best ways you can collaborate on this adventure.

Take full responsibility for Team You, by holding yourself accountable in a positive way for everything you do. Instead of regretting a mistake, find out what you need to do differently and do that.

Who you are is a story told by many, including yourself. Feeling good about yourself relies on defining yourself as a work of art in progress rather than an outcome. Find a balance between feeling great about what you already are and being able to improve. You are always enough and evolving.

Essence

" *You are a process of enoughness*

in evolution. **"**

Explore Your Narrative

Fill in the blanks and make these claims aloud:

1. I am _____.

2. Apart from this, I am also _____.

3. Beyond this, I am not _____.

4. A different belief would stop me from _____.

5. A different belief would allow me to _____.

Just add water and practice, a lot of practice.

~ Don T. Bidoux

BOTTOM LINE:
YOU ARE THE CREATOR

Your personality is a dish of experiences, beliefs, and habits served in situations to whoever is at the table.

Create the creator: Imagination offers you an ocean of possibilities. Get wet.

Your symphony: The symphony of you evolves through the instruments, the acoustics, the audience, and the way the music is directed.

Enough already: You are a process of enoughness in evolution.

YOU'VE GOT THE POWER

O nce you grab the steering wheel, your interaction
with life evolves into what to change and how.

Good vibrations can
walk like an Egyptian and
surprise yourself;
for whom the bell tolls.
Maximus meets Satisfix, so
receive and thou shalt give
and if nothing else helps, laugh!

GOOD VIBRATIONS

People say nothing is impossible, but I do it every day.

~ Theodor Rosyfelt, *The Foolish Almanak for Anuthur Year*

It is the ultimate spark of life. It lies dormant in every action and perspective. It can be created in any form of action, as simple as returning a smile, as complex as raising a child. It can be found in the wings of a butterfly.

You are washed in a river of meetings every moment, and there are many ways to swim. In theory, every living being you encounter has a potential key to the total meaning of your life.

There is a mystic relationship of meaning between work, materialistic achievement, and social fun. It is a dance between pain and gain. There is meaning in traditions and rituals; there is meaning in stepping outside that box. There is meaning in failure, there is meaning in success. You can find meaning in a good meal, a new pair of shoes, and a job well done. There can also be meaning in taking a day off doing absolutely nothing, hanging out with a friend and climbing a tree.

Meaning is everywhere, and for you to create. In loss, grief, and pain, look for a meaning waiting to help you grow. Meaning is personal. Everything changes meaning depending on the story you choose to tell about it.

There are multiple dimensions of meaning. The meaning of an experience and a meaning looking back at it. Missing a bus may lead to meeting the love of your life. Some say having an accident or experiencing a loss woke them up and reminded them of how valuable life was all along. With the right meaning, incredible efforts can be carried with a smile.

Essence

66 *Imagine meaning to be something
you create.* 99

Explore Your Meanings

Look for the meaning beyond the obvious meaning in something that happens.

Explore Your Awe

When was the last time you felt awe, and what made it happen?

What you imagine is possible.

~ Don T. Bidoux

WALK LIKE AN EGYPTIAN

*In matters of style, swim with the current; in matters
of principle, flow like a rock.*

~ trad/arr

Even if a dance can be taught as separate steps, the potential of the dance lies in honoring its principles and adding elegance to the process.

When songwriter Liam Sternberg watched people adapting to the movement patterns of a ferry negotiating rocky water, he noticed that they developed an awkward but ingenious way of walking to keep their balance. Their poses reminded him of figures in ancient Egyptian paintings. They probably didn't think much of it themselves, but they had found a walking strategy to cope with the principles of unsteady ground. In fact, every unsteady ground you have encountered has developed your toolbox of strategies.

Your decisions and actions are guided by strategies and there is no known limit to how many you can have. One situation may call for being more introverted, another more extroverted.

These kinds of strategies are not in your genes; they are tools of mind that you can develop into useful behaviors.

Most of the advice and books about becoming skilled in an area of life are about strategies. Business strategies, health strategies, relationship strategies, even strategies for luck. One strategy of lucky people is that they hold their heads higher, which allows them to notice a lucky moment when it appears.

Strategies are a mix of attitude and how that can be applied from one area of life to another. From the world of chess there is a saying, *"Play the board and not the player"*; from the world of magic, *"Look where you want the audience to look"*; and from the art of war, *"Victorious warriors win first and then go to war"* as said by Sun Tzu in The Art of War a couple of thousand years ago.

A central strategy of life is that of win or play. *To win* is to care about yourself, because it is important that you win, even beyond having fun. Because of this, you will be strategic at all times. *To play* is to care about everyone. It is less important who wins, because having fun is your goal, and because of this, you can be authentic all the time.

The art and elegance of a flexible mindset are to cultivate your strategies. Whenever you get a result more than twice, look for an unconscious strategy behind the curtains. Make it a habit to identify useful strategies, the general ones, and the specific ones. Ask yourself if you are playing to win, to have fun, or a combination.

Essence

“ *Every process has an underlying principle, out of which that flower grows. Strategies are the software of successful gardening.* ”

Explore Your Strategies

Look at a specific situation where you get a specific result that you wish were different:

1. Look at the steps you had to take to get there.

2. Look at the thoughts and values motivating each of those steps.

3. Compare them to other steps you take, with better and similar results.

4. Change something, and explore the difference.

Anytime you see a turtle on a fence, you know it had some help.

~ Traditional saying often attributed to Alex Haley, an important author

SURPRISE YOURSELF

You are born into an amazing machine with
incredible abilities and no manual. Do you have
any idea, what you are capable of?

~ Don T. Bidoux

The part of you reading this is a self-regenerating, self-programming, multidimensional supercomputer and survival system. The extreme spectrum of what you are capable of learning and doing is quite impressive, often surprising in ways you may already know.

The very memory you are using to remember this can be doubled in a short time, with training. You have yet to explore the actual boundaries of what you are capable of remembering. For sure, it is probably more than you can keep in mind.

We tend to believe that our brain is the center of our consciousness, yet there is no conclusive proof, because your intelligence seems to be spread throughout your body, maybe even beyond. Medical science can attest that some people that had large parts of their physical brain removed have continued to live with most of their personalities and skills intact, including becoming chess and bowling champions. Imagine that, and ask what part of you is doing it, and what part is answering this question.

Every one of your actions uses energy in some form. This energy requires hormones, amino acids, minerals, and oxygen; and regenerates you into a new you, on a cellular level, triggering a process by which new neurons are created in your brain. This is fueled throughout life by interaction with other humans all the way to the act of making love, a hormone inducing action proven to promote neurogenesis.

While you may have been told that you have limits as to what you can do at the same time, at the same time you can, once you have trained yourself to do so. You have many ways of thinking, different senses, thinking in sounds and words, and images, and body sensations. You can walk and talk and think as long as you separate the processes. Two dialogues at the same time seem to be more of a challenge.

The surprising abilities that a human brain is capable of include extreme memory; extraordinary musical talent, mechanical, and spatial skills; intriguing calendar and math calculations; and other incredible computing skills. Most people can spot a repeated image of thousands after seeing them for a few minutes. It can come up with an idea of putting man on the moon and then make it happen, and realize something without being able to explain how you do.

Essence

❝ *Nobody knows what you are*

capable of. Be the first to

find out. ❞

Explore a change of Breath

1. Sit down, take a deep, deep breath, and hold it.
2. Notice how your lungs shift your posture.
3. Relax your body around your lungs.
4. Breathe out sounding the letter "f" and notice how the weight of your body increases.
5. Repeat twice.
6. Allow your eyes to gaze into space without focus.
7. Put a small smile on your face and notice what happens to your facial muscles.
8. Close your eyes and notice what happens if you keep breathing like this for a while.

Explore Choices

The next time you are doing something, anything at all, say this out loud:

"Right now I choose to _____ because _____ and I could also choose to _____."

Explore Limitations

If you first process a lot of information and then do something remarkably different, you will be able to access your intuitive thinking on what you processed earlier.

Spend a short time focusing intensely on a situation or decision.

Stop.

Skip to a remarkably unrelated activity for a short time.

Go back to the subject.

You are a function of what the whole universe is doing in the same way that a wave is a function of what the whole ocean is doing.

~ Alan Watts

FOR WHOM THE BELL TOLLS

"There are three kinds of lies: lies, damned lies, and statistics.

~ Popularized by Samuel Langhorne Clemens, writer and humorist

The power of predicting the future seems to lie in observations and statistics from the past. However, if you sit in a train at a station and see another train move outside the window, you will not know if your train or the other is in motion.

When you base your actions on the probability of success, you are using a reference point for the expected result, a norm. This is an important use of science, to observe the cause and effect of a process and to create a bell curve for expected, normal behaviors and reactions. The bell curve illustrates how the results of an action will affect most people, those in the middle of the curve. At the far left and far right are the exceptions to this norm, the outliers.

If a probability applies to most people, it may apply to you. Unless, of course, you are one of the outliers. Then this bell does not toll for you. At all. If one percent survives a medical condition beyond probability, focus on what they did and do it. If anybody else has succeeded beyond odds in a situation similar to yours, make sure you are the next one. If nobody has done it before you, be the first one.

A part of you is creating a personal bell curve to predict your next action. Every statistic, norm, and observation is a dish from the past, so consume it with care.

What if

- you are more than your beliefs
- you are more than your social class or your health
- you are more than your history
- you are more than the average of some statistics
- you are more than every potential expression of your genes
- you are more than your story, or anybody else's

Essence

66 *Society's illusion of normalcy is based on averages of others in the past. Don't let it stop you.* 99

Explore the Limits of Your Beliefs

What is a belief you would like to hold because it will make you explore a dream?

What would you need to experience to be able to hold it?

Luck is what happens when preparation meets opportunity.

~ Seneca, Roman philosopher

MAXIMUS MEETS SATISFIX

Whatever the Thinker thinks, the Prover proves.

~ Robert Anton Wilson,
Prometheus Rising

A skilled sailor seeks to reach a destination by navigating with the trip and the goal equally in mind. The waves may agree or not.

Some will navigate under the flag of an unattainable perfectionism, grimly accomplishing masterful goals. However, at the finish line, many realize that the journey, the smiles, the shared moments and stories are the memorable meaning beyond that, which is not for real.

How is one to know, when the tone of the guitar matters more than the melody, because sometimes the highest standards are an inevitable part of a great result. It is however rare, and more often the case, that *perfect* is more about *good enough* in every part, for the excellence of the whole.

If the process is enjoyed and embraced at the highest standards of what is actually possible in the given circumstances, and no less, there can be no regret, other than that of being in these circumstances. *Well done* is done as well as it can, remembering the higher meaning and the fulfilment from the experience itself. This seems to be the true perfection beyond perfection. That which can be done with a smile and looked back upon as a great memory.

In the winds of life, your sails can be trimmed by Maximus and Satisfix, and when you navigate, you need to ask if it is the speed of the boat, the perfect direction or the most enjoyable trip you are looking for. A dream can be embellished with multiple dreams on its way, allowing destinations unforeseen.

Maximus trims the sails strongly in the direction of making the best choices, avoids every mistake, and looks for perfection regardless of costs. Sometimes this may be the best thing to do; other times less so.

Satisfix seeks to playfully paint the bigger picture with alternative goals, creating an enjoyable ride where the company can relax into a smooth process that can make a great tale.

Both approaches may involve the highest standards possible.

Essence

> **Wherever the wind blows, there is a choice to navigate.**

Explore Alternative Perfection

During the next three days, explore how you can make your bed closer to your idea of playful perfection every morning; what principles are involved; and what kind of perfection you regard as joyful, useful, and well done. Explore alternative strategies and resources. Embrace different ways of processing it.

Explore the Choice of Not Choosing

The next time you are choosing between two options, Maximize one of them, Satisfy the other. If possible, both.

You cannot be better or worse than anyone else. Do the best that you can be, that's all.

~ Don T. Bidoux

RECEIVE AND THOU SHALT GIVE

Maybe it's the same soup.

~ Don T. Bidoux

Consider the metaphorical difference between repro-ducing, having sex, and making love. The intention of a gift is an energy different from the actual gift.

To accept a gift is a gift in itself, sometimes bigger than the gift. When you ask somebody for a favor they will instinc-tively like you, for obviously your taste is impeccable. In fact, accepting a gift makes you more likable than giving it.

How surprised is the cat dropping a dead bird at your feet if you don't enjoy it, or the mud pie of a child. A gift unre-ceived is a sorrow for all involved. There is no need to fake enjoyment. Simply honour the intention: "What a lovely thing to do for somebody. Thank you, thank you, thank you." At the same time, the size of a gift bears little or no relation to the joy it may bring to both when accepted. Offer a glass of water or a smile, and explore.

There is a difference between being strong and being stubborn. Sometimes admitting weakness is the strongest thing you can do. In extreme situations, knowing when to ask for help and accepting support can be what keeps you and others alive. While for some there may be a fear of being in debt, there is always the possibility of paying it forward instead.

The language of love and friendship is that of actions intended to show affection and care. It is a stream of gifts flowing in both directions, sometimes under the radar of the other. While one prefers the gift of care in words, the other may prefer a hand on the shoulder or a flower on the doorstep.

Among the magical qualities of gifts is the power of giving kindly to somebody you have no relationship with, someone who will never find out this gift was from you. Paying it forward.

Essence

66 *Accepting a gift empowers the person giving it. Win-win.* 99

Explore the Love of Receiving

Honor the intent of a favor you may not need. Explore how many small gifts you can receive in a day, and what happens to the giver when you do.

Pay Something Forward

Think of a gift or favor somebody gave you, and do something similar for somebody you do not know or who doesn't expect it. Notice what happens if they accept it, or not.

It's in front of us, and nobody understands it,
including ourselves.

~ Don T. Bidoux

IF NOTHING ELSE HELPS, LAUGH!

Sometimes people say, 'One day you are going to look back at this and laugh.' My question is 'Why wait?' "

~ Richard Bandler,
pioneer of tranceformation

It lives in your body, and something can wake it up. Some say a good laugh leaves a footprint in the soul: go inside and look for laughter, one you remember or wish to. Nurture it and teach it to enjoy yourself in a curious and playful way. Smile when you remember your face. Look not for a reason to laugh; laugh as a reason to live.

And as you do, some part of you will remember that our survival as a species is an act of collaboration. We are creatures of flock and can best herd laughter out loud in the company of someone else. If we were meant to have more fun alone, everybody would be able to tickle themselves to tears of joy. As a matter of fact, very few can lick their elbows too, and only some try.

Looking at a flood, even at a small creek, can be calming, fascinating, and enjoyable.

There seems to be a certain humor in how it will smile its way past any obstacle placed in its way, as if saying that this, too, has a funny side. How little strength it displays, yet how powerful it can be. The laughter isn't the water itself; it is how it moves and from where it bubbles. There is a trickle, a splash, a squirt, and more.

Once upon a modern time there was a man diagnosed with an incurable disease. He was told his days were counted, so he created a room of healing, in which he collected vitamins, good friends, and funny movies. By laughing daily for months, he cured himself and lived happily ever after.

Should you find yourself in a dark void of the soul, look for that small sign of a noteworthy absurdity, something that might bring a smile around the campfires of the future, then soar above like a soaring bird, and smile, maybe even laugh, from a distance. Some call it a mocking bird for a reason...

Now look inside again, as you can, and search in places you didn't know you could, find it, that fountain from where your untamed laughter emerges when you aren't prepared, when you don't need to be. Explore how your body prepares for it, if it is a shift in your muscles or your breathing. And how suddenly it may spread on its way to the surface of your face. Notice the temperature if you spin it in whatever way you find inappropriate, and while some need a unicorn or a rabbit, you may be different. How many flavors of joy can you detect in a scoop of it; bubbling, slowly emerging in the way only you can allow, and couldn't stop even if you tried. Notice what it does to your body, when it reaches the corners of your lips and eyes. What else is there, about laughter?

Essence

> *Laughter seems to evolve naturally where the seriousness of life takes a break.*

Spread Your Laughter

Laugh in the unexpected and see how many you can get to join in.

Explore Somebody Else's Laughter

Next time you hear one or more people laughing aloud, listen carefully and notice what you realize.

We had nothing, but we decided to laugh because it felt so much better.

~ Placide Nkubito,
master of enoughness

BOTTOM LINE:
YOU'VE GOT THE POWER

Your power boils down to doing what is meaningful, knowing when to keep moving, what to change and how.

Good vibrations: Imagine meaning to be something you create.

Walk like an Egyptian: Every process has an underlying principle, out of which that flower grows. Strategies are the software of successful gardening.

Surprise yourself: Nobody knows what you are capable of, be the first to find out.

For whom the bell tolls: Society's illusion of normalcy is based on averages of others in the past. Don't let it stop you.

Maximus meets Satisfix: Wherever the wind blows, there is a choice to navigate.

Receive and Thou shalt give: Accepting a gift empowers the person giving it. Win-win.

If nothing else helps, laugh! Laughter seems to evolve naturally where the seriousness of life takes a break.

IT'S ACTUALLY QUITE SIMPLE

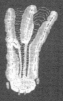

*The scientists climbed the mountain and found
the mystics waiting there.*

~ trad/arr

Your body is a fundamental condition for your existence. In order to survive and thrive it will produce urges of hunger, thirst, intimacy, activity, and sleep. Inside your body your genes are interacting with an overlapping mission to adapt and replicate.

Your mind is working around the clock to create, understand, and explain your life experience. It cooperates most of the time with the needs of your body to maintain comfort. Beyond your practical mind is a part of you that yearns to evolve and to connect with others through humor, art, play, and love in the search of a higher, sometimes undefinable meaning.

Your mind wants to understand; your body wants to survive and thrive; your genes want to adapt and replicate; and your soul wants to evolve, connect, and express itself. When these dimensions are in tune and aligned you can choose what songs to play.

Your Happy Gene supports your
Soul Survival, and your
Mushroom Personality, so
Tune Your Tentacles and create
a Mind of Your Own, to bloom, also in the
company of Everything But You.

YOUR HAPPY GENE

Life and the brain evolved to feel good

~ Stuart Hameroff,
from *The Quantum Origin of life*

Your genetic hand was dealt thousands of years ago. It is a magical box of possible expressions accumulated from many sources.

Gene expression is when your circumstances cause your cells to ask your DNA to retrieve one of millions of possible reactions, traits, and evolutionary patterns stored in your gene bank. When nothing is asked, nothing is retrieved, which means that you are less predestined by your genes than is a person walking into a library predestined to borrow a specific book.

Your genes will listen and react to your living conditions. The mechanics and chemistry of your environment will speak directly to them, as will the interaction between the nutrition, the amino acids, and the proteins as you eat.

It's not only where you are and what you do, it's also how you feel about it. If you believe there is a monster under your bed, you will raise your heartbeat, produce adrenaline and cortisol and other fight-and-flight hormones. This will signal to your cells that there is danger. The danger signals will be sent to your DNA. This can lead to your genes expressing themselves to fight the monster in your mind.

When your mind shines a sun of meaning over whatever happens to you, it will counter your genetic reactions to the circumstances under which your life plays out. In fact, a positive mind looking through the lens of gratitude and positive thinking can be a conditioner for your cell health, because, in the pool of life's social mirror neurons, the water of hope is a shared resource, be it yours or that of the people surrounding you.

As you travel the road of a possible partnership, your genes will be in the backseat giving you directions for what they believe to be in their interest of survival or replication. Your genes may want you to have babies with people that you have little else in common with, as long as their mission to reproduce is accomplished. However vital they are in the agenda of gene replication, both attraction and sex have dimensions of emotional regulation and a consolidation of partnerships of the soul. Your genes are one part of this fascinating dance.

The information in your DNA has accumulated over millions of years. Taking care of your body where this information lives and the environment your body interacts with allows your genes to express their best for you. Your thoughts are in constant dialogue with your genes about what song to play. Roll out a red carpet and trust them to sing the better songs.

Essence

❝ *Your genes are a rainbow of possibilities dancing with your thoughts and environment.* **❞**

Explore the Possible

Pick any aspect of your health or wellbeing that may, or may not, be related to your genetics. Ask yourself, "What if it is?"

What will you do differently?

Pick the same aspect and ask yourself, "What if it isn't?"

What will you do differently?

Belief and reality create each other.

~ Don T. Bidoux

SOUL SURVIVAL

Hope is being happy now about being happy then

~ Don T. Bidoux

You can use a glass mirror to see your face and you can use works of art to see your soul. Art opens doors to passion, spirituality, and connection. The art of nature in the simple form of a sunset can cause part of you to vibrate with awe and joy. They happen every day and we should line up to see them. What is this about?

Behind everything you do there is an urge or need. People have found meaning in the face of death, in times of need, hunger, involuntary social isolation, and danger. Your genes have a need to adapt and replicate; your body has a need to survive and thrive; your soul wants to connect and express itself; and your mind has a need to understand. The want of them, is where you are heading, this very moment. The need of them, is what lies underneath.

In the adventure of exploring you and the cultural garden you are grown from, you may regard the source of these wants as something beyond your body and mind. Putting words on it can be like trying to hug a dolphin in a sea of olive oil, while the waves seek to become your friends. It cannot be ignored any more than having a butterfly on your nose and acting like it's not there. It is a part of you beyond you that may have been there even before you were. For some it is a fairy tale and for some it is more real than the ground under your feet. In each case it will be up to you.

As you explore the souls around you, you may find them lost, happy, young, old, or just soulful, full of that mystic ingredient that makes it so. When you meet somebody whose soul vibrates in congruence with your own, you may call it kindred, and in some cases even a mate.

If you approach the questions of eternity, existence, and your soul from the curious perspective of somebody never indoctrinated about it, you may wonder whether you exist prior to your birth and after. If you are connected to a larger system in the now or in the beyond. If you recycle and reincarnate or not. If "you" are a chemical, biological phenomenon, or a part of something divine. The meaning of the journey, the connection of everything. Spirituality, religion, philosophy, and science offer you boats to sail these seas.

Maybe the whole world is a living organism and you are a part of this organism. When you interact with art, nature, and other people, something happens to everything.

A balance or imbalance in your soul will express itself in your body and mind. Any attempt to numb these messages with medication is like turning down the volume of a radio during an important news broadcast. *Psyche* means "soul"; *psychotherapy* means "healing of the soul." Awakening and developing this mystical part of you can be as simple as dedicating some time and effort to connect with others and playfully explore art and questions posed by eternity. Life is a condition that allows you to experience this extraordinary dimension of you. Honor it.

Essence

" *A part of you needs to resonate with art, ideas, nature, and something beyond time and space.* **"**

Explore Your Soul

If you were to increase the wellbeing of your soul one breath a day, what will you do differently?

Explore Somebody Else's Soul

Define the essence of the soul of another living being without words.

Explore Ideas of Soul

Here are some ideas about soul interpreted freely.

Your soul is like a bridge between your spiritual planetary body and your physical body here. The task for your soul is to understand and to let this understanding guide you on your way.

~ Taoism interpreted

God will breathe your soul into your body when you are in your mothers womb. Once you die it will be kept on hold until judgement day, at which your actions will be revised and you will be sent to heaven or hell.

~ The essence of words spoken
in the Islamic faith

Your mission is to evolve and mature through your experiences and choices as your contribution to the soul of the world.

~ The ancient Upanishads interpreted

Your soul is born with your body and evolves throughout your life. It is everything that makes you individually unique. Your soul is connected to the collective soul of humanity.

~ Ancient Egyptian beliefs interpreted

Your soul can be reborn several times to fulfill its mission in life, after which it is kept for resurrection at a later point into heaven or hell.

~ Interpretation of beliefs practiced in Judaism

Your soul is immortal, it comes with a mission and returns to be evaluated. It has three simultaneous dimensions: your soul to be born, your soul of life and your soul of after-life. It is unclear how many missions you get.

~ Interpretation of beliefs practiced by the Yoruba people

Your soul manifests in one life as the image of God and leaves your body when you die to be judged and resurrected into heaven or hell.

~ *Interpretation* of beliefs practiced in Christianity

Your soul is an eternal entity interacting with your physical organism (your body and mind) and will therefore continue to exist after your body ceases to.

~ The essence of words spoken by Plato

Your soul is not proven to exist.

> ~ The essence of skeptical pragmatism

The goal of your life is to attain wisdom beyond the physical temptations and challenges of your body, your senses, your emotions, your feelings, and your awareness of them.

> ~ Interpretation of beliefs encountered in Buddhism

In the face of life, assume not, explore.

~ Don T. Bidoux

MUSHROOM PERSONALITY

I'm growing mushrooms ... they just keep multiplying ... and it's like ... I'm in service to them.

~ Sharon Weil, from Donny and Ursula Save the World

There is an undeniable perfection in the ecological dance of organisms in a coral reef, and it happens by itself, given the time and peace to evolve. In the same way, it is amazing how we humans can create cities and towns all over the world where you are sure to find a hairdresser, a baker, and a doctor.

In a similar way, your mind and sense of self depend on an incredible collaboration among the cells and microscopic organisms that make up your body. Some of your cells are regenerated in days, some in months, and some every number of years; a reincarnating circus where some very small parts, such as the cells of the lenses in your eyes, stay the same during the whole adventure.

A major part of this daily reincarnation relies on how happy you keep the metropolis of your microbiome. Your gut is host to a highly specialized society of over 100 trillion microorganisms that transform your food so that your body can use it to regenerate yourself and maintain your immune system. It's a rather amazing collaboration going on around the clock, which dances to the sum of what you eat and in what form, accompanied by how you sleep, exercise, fraternize, laugh, and expose yourself to light.

If your mind is the stage on which your life unfolds, the balance of your gut is the capacity of the theater, and the amount of thoughts and dreams you can seat. Feel-good hormones and vital brain juices such as serotonin are manufactured in your gut, so make sure your mushroom community is thriving. Remember to feed your soul and your body; sometimes something sweet can put a smile on your face while too much can foster aggression and unrest. Eat well to feel well to think well.

What seems to be the government lives behind the curtain of your eyes and uses a significant portion of your energy. Thinking in itself will take a toll on your metabolism; solving math can be more exhausting than playing with a puppy. Despite this, your heart has been shown to communicate more with your mind than the other way around. At the same time the collaboration of the gut can affect all of them. Simply put, there is a collaboration, a team that needs to sing the same tune. You are living in a mammal: treat it with respect.

These amazing cycles have evolved from a million year flood of minerals, vitamins, proteins, and amino acids finding their way with enough fiber to transport it through your mushroom factory and enough mechanical energy to distribute them into your bloodstream and carry away the waste. The diet you decide your mammal should tolerate may not be in tune with its needs, and often it will tell you if you listen closely enough.

At any given moment you are a collaboration of communities, including bacteria and fungi. Any imbalance will reflect who you seem to be. Simple principles of wellbeing have been known for thousands of years. They give better odds of a long, healthy, and meaningful life than any hack, wonder pill, or symptom fix yet invented.

A great composer once said that it is the pause between the notes that separates music from noise. In the same way there are many, well-sung benefits of allowing your metropolis to pause in different ways. Even the ocean waits a moment before the next wave.

On a higher level, your amazing collaboration of cells and mushrooms are dancing to the vibrations of your environment and thoughts, the energy and the people around you.

The tune played on a harp is not the harp, but they depend on each other. As you explore every other aspect of your life, your personality and your unleashed potential, make sure you have found your mix of rest, hydration, social interaction, exercise, and the presence or absence of food and drugs in every form. You are the sum. Be the sum.

Essence

66 *Your feelings, thoughts, and physical health are a collaboration with millions of unseen communities. Collaborate with respect and love.* 99

Explore the Obvious

If you (can) avoid sugar, white flour, milk, and gluten more often than not, most metabolisms are known to cheer. Your system depends on biochemical fuels such as unsaturated fatty acids, zinc, magnesium, iron, folate, and the vitamins. Read up and fuel up. What can you do differently to improve this collaboration by the size of a breath, each day, this week?

Explore the Fast Track

From water fasting to intermittent fasting or calorie restriction, there are enough types of fasting to fit any lifestyle.

A Note on the Unique Biology of Women

As a woman, your moods will be influenced by the ebb and flood or your hormonal cycles, the very same machinery that makes it possible for you to produce new life. This dance starts before your first period and evolves throughout life. It can be quite a roller coaster that runs on the tracks of overall life stress. When the balance of modern life sets the speed of the roller coaster higher than the track is built for, your behaviors, thoughts, and moods can change radically. Learn more about it. Scientific research is finally looking into it.

There is an intelligence in every one of us that can turn a banana or a piece of bread into a human being.

~ Sadhguru, founder of Isha Foundation

TUNE YOUR TENTACLES

What you do affects everything, the future of this world depends on it.

~ Don T. Bidoux

You are connected to the world through an amazing web of tentacles collecting information for you to act upon through your senses. At any given moment, millions of pieces of information about your environment, body status, and beliefs create a wave of possible actions for you to surf.

The dialogue that goes on beyond consciousness is juggling split-second decisions and long-term goals with the grace of an octopus. Some tentacles are wired into your needs of food and rest all the way down to instructing your cells and immune system. Some are judging the safety of your environment, ready to push you into fight or flight if necessary. Others are looking for something pleasant to experience and people you can experience it with. With so much information, it's quite amazing how you can choose what to do, in any given moment.

Your sense of touch allows you to perceive temperature, pressure, and friction. You also have an ability to maintain balance and to know where your body parts are in any given moment, which provides a kinesthetic realm that can be set to an offline mode so your mind can dream you are running, while in fact you are very still.

Smell and taste go hand in hand, both handling chemical molecules, guiding your preferences in food, but also sensing fear, lust, illness, and perspiration from people around you. In addition, your mind invites information from your body functions, and their interactions with acceleration, gravity, and time. For every sensation detected, part of your mind creates a meaning, a resident storyteller around the campfire of your thoughts.

Some of your tentacles collect temperature, sound, light, and smell. Other tentacles check the status of your environment and body functions, even beyond your awareness, and there are tentacles that reach into the past by looking through the lenses of your memories and past experiences. You also look into the future using your imagination, based on previous experiences and beliefs. It's a multidimensional, ongoing navigational process looking to explore life in the best ways possible.

Birds are probably unaware that they use magnetic fields to navigate, and in the same way you are using a web of tentacles without knowing that you do. If you experience information coming to your mind from what seems to be nowhere, you may call it premonition or intuition. Having a hunch that you should connect to a person you haven't talked to in a while and then finding out it was mutual is an everyday example of how you can obtain information in unexplainable ways, sense things in distant places, and be affected by them.

If you can notice it, identify it, and imagine what it can lead to, you can act upon it. The trick is to tune into what is most relevant, filter out the rest, not get overwhelmed, and enjoy the ride.

Essence

> **You have extraordinary senses for interacting with the world, of which you probably only have discovered a fraction.**

Explore

1. Keep your eyes open, yet stop looking at anything specific except this text.

2. Keep your eyes almost shut, almost closed, and notice the difference in your mind.

3. Start a micro-dancing movement of your shoulders in slow motion.

4. Listen to your environment, then to your body.

5. What is that taste in your mouth, and where does it change?

6. How much of your skin can you become aware of?

7. Notice how heavy you can become, and what gravity does to keep you from floating into space?

8. And as you do, disregard what you know about a person, anybody, and use anything but your rational mind to understand them, right now.

Make no friendship with an elephant keeper if you have no room to entertain an elephant.

~ Saadi

A MIND OF YOUR OWN

*Don't be satisfied with stories, how things have gone
with others. Unfold your own myth.*

~ Rumi

It's there in your head as soon as you wake up and thoughts can be created intentionally or they can sail into it from somewhere. Part of it is obvious and some of it seems to happen beyond the horizon of consciousness. Your mind is helping you make sense of these words, of everything, right now.

As life dances through your window of consciousness, your mind looks to make sense of it, deciding how you should react. Your specific life experience is unique, one of a kind, and, therefore, so are you. There is one map of the world for every individual creating it. Even as you read this, part of your mind can go "is there?" or "that's right." When somebody else is hard to understand, remember that their map is different from yours. It can be no other way.

Whatever your mind allows you to think will be possible in your mind. Putting men on the moon or growing roses start as ideas and become actions. Every single human innovation started in a mind just like yours. Imagine.

Your mind will do everything it can to help you survive, and to bring joy, meaning, and pleasure to your life. Every experience brings information that your mind will sort and store for future use. To help you to accumulate experiences and refine your actions, your mind creates memories. To work with them, you have skills like pattern recognition, generalizations, cause and effect observations, and equivalences.

Your ability to recognize patterns helps you identify concepts; for example, recognizing that a bottle is a bottle, even if bottles can be shaped in thousands of ways. Once you put words on something you can describe it to another person as a generalized concept, but to imagine it, their mind will look for an example out of their own experience. You say, "dog" to somebody and your two minds will agree on the concept even though the image in each mind is a different size and breed.

The thoughts in your mind are invited by circumstances: there are intentional thoughts, realizations, unwelcome thoughts, and stillness. Thoughts even seem to have a mind of their own. If you summon the thought of an apple without defining it, your mind will provide a color, probably red or green, a texture, and a size for you. You might remember what it feels like to hold an apple, to recall the sound of biting into it or its taste. Every one of your senses has an apple experience to tell.

Since your mind is so keen on making sense of things, it can trip over itself trying to do so. Once it decides something is true, it will look to prove it in every way possible, maybe even by filtering out anything that points in a different direction.

There are two major mindsets that will shift the functioning of your thoughts; if you are looking for what to avoid out of fear and lack; or if you are looking for solutions and possibilities out of curiosity, playfulness, and a lust for experiencing life. There is a third mindset in the face of danger: which is that of immediate survival, during which most of the thinking mind is somewhere else. The mindset you exercise will grow more than the other two.

As you explore the dimensions of your mind, you will find that your logical thinking is a wonderful instrument for organizing, deconstructing, and sorting the parts of life that are logical. Since a vast portion of life doesn't follow logic, your mind also uses intuition.

The intuitive part of your mind can work incredibly fast, connecting facts and ideas beyond the restrictions of what is explainable in words and logic. Once it comes to a conclusion, it will ring a bell giving you a gut feeling or an "aha!" moment, bringing the conclusion to the rest of your mind.

Your mind is not limited to you. When musicians, dancers, or sport teams perform organically they can behave as bees in a beehive with a united awareness.

Your emotions and perceptions of the world are processed as thoughts, and brought to your awareness. Your awareness is a window of consciousness into your mind's theater where imagination and reality meet.

Essence

" The tools that your mind is using right now to make sense of your life and the world around you are amazing. Don't let them fool you. "

Explore Dream Logic

As you may have noticed, a part of your imagination can stay up and create dreams beyond your daily logic when the rest of you goes to sleep. Before you enter the world of dreams, give that part of your mind a task, a question about something creative, and allow it to spend the night solving it in its own ways.

Say to yourself: "Tonight, as I dream, I wish a part of me will come up with inspiration and possible solutions for _____."

Use Dream Logic for Life

Next time you find yourself in a situation you wish to understand, explore it with dream logic: "If this situation were a dream, what message would it carry for me?"

Explore Systemic Consciousness

As you speak to somebody, imagine a third mind that is the combination of you both, a bubble in which both of you enter temporarily. What is ... it ... like?

Step Out of Your Slow Mind

Next time you have a task that seems hard to solve or grasp, go over it faster than you think possible all the way to the end. Leave it, do something else, and then return a second time to go over it and see what has changed.

Explore Your Sorting

Usually your mind will sort life into categories, stored geographically in the theatre of your mind. Close your eyes and explore the difference in how your mind thinks of something great and something you are completely uninterested in. Where is each located and how far away from you are they?

Quack!

~ trad/arr

EVERYTHING BUT YOU

I am very short-sighted, and if I don't like a situa-
tion, I take my glasses off.

~ Jenny Eclair, comedian

Take a step back and consider yourself. The dynamics of who you are capable of being is an interaction with the acoustics of the ocean you are swimming in. Everything but you is also a part of what brings out the possible in you.

Your environment offers invisible vibrations, chemicals, and electromagnetic forces contributing to the sum of your physical performance and wellbeing. Exercising high above the level of the sea will allow your body to handle oxygen in a different way, and your exposure to the frequency of a certain color, can increase your creativity. Bathing in nature can wash away stress as well as dust, and open a doorway to the greater you. The song of every chemical compound, mechanical vibration, and microorganism will change the acoustics of your symphony. To explore yourself, explore the world. There is another you on every mountain top, in every valley, tree, and stream.

Every person has something to teach you about yourself, providing billions of potential chapters in the book of you. You have something in common with every other creature on this planet, and they all know something else, for you to find out.

In Rwanda, the land of a thousand hills, milk, and honey, there is a saying that every human has a precious pearl inside, and that to discover it we need to see it through the eyes of somebody else; Ikirezi. Has somebody found yours yet?

You are playing a tune involving every other living organism in your field of existence. Over time you will absorb qualities of the environment you spend the most time in. A team is a tune of many notes, and sometimes one too many. The you beyond you involves the world. What can it help you become and how can you assist it to evolve?

Essence

66 *Your potential is the how that vibrates with your where, why, and who.* 99

Explore Your Company

In every meeting, choose to interact in a way that resonates with the company you would prefer. Be that company.

Enhance Your Environment

Explore a minor, subtle, or extravagant change in one of your daily environments. Put a new flower where you sleep, wear a new color, offer a stranger a three-course meal.

Explore Your Global Impact

Imagine the world improving in a way that would make you happy. What would you do differently? Be the first to do it.

Be genuinely interested in the other person. Smile like you mean it. Remember their name, and know that it is to that person the sweetest and most important sound in any language. Be a good listener and talk in terms of their interests. Make them feel important—and do it sincerely.

~ Dale Carnegie

BOTTOM LINE:
IT'S ACTUALLY QUITE SIMPLE

Sometimes the big questions are the small ones.

Your happy gene: Your genes are a rainbow of possibilities dancing with your thoughts and environment.

Soul survival: A part of you needs to resonate with art, ideas, nature and something beyond time and space.

Mushroom personality: Your feelings, thoughts and physical health are a collaboration with millions of unseen communities. Collaborate with respect and love.

Tune your tentacles: You have extraordinary senses for interacting with the world, of which you probably only have discovered a fraction.

A mind of your own: The tools that your mind is using right now to make sense of your life and the world around you are amazing. Don't let them fool you.

Everything but you: Your potential is the how that vibrates with your where, why, and who.

THE MENU
IS NOT THE MEAL

You are driven by principles and beliefs about what is possible and what to expect, a paradigm. When a paradigm changes, everything changes.

*Let's all make beliefs and
memories of you, for a
curse or blessing is in the eye of the beholder.*

LET'S ALL MAKE BELIEFS

Beliefs have shaped the very sofa on which I sit.

~ Inspired by the words of Mason Cooley,
master of aphorisms

They are the wind in the sails of your actions, the source of your morals and self-esteem. You can create beliefs, inherit them, put words on them and dress them in metaphors. Some will parade at the front of your mind while others dance in the background of your subconscious. The nature of your beliefs is the nature of everything you experience. Your actions, your identity, and your reality are based on your beliefs.

In the limitless garden of beliefs there are no boundaries. You can find religion and love blooming without contradiction in pastures of science and common sense. At the table of shared beliefs, you will find kindred minds with aligned norms and values. They will grow from what you believe you know, and then believe you know. They will bloom into your values and actions.

Every belief can be translated into a metaphor, and while the metaphor tells you about your belief, changing it can allow you to change your belief as simply as creating a door in a wall.

You can believe in parallel dimensions and afterlife using the same wonderful tool that allows you to believe there are clothes on your body right now. Beliefs have put man on the moon. They are the fabric of hope, faith, meaning, entitlement, justice, science, and friendship. They allow your mind to build temples with bricks of logic held together by clay of imagination. Ideas like money, marriage, and morals cease to exist without them. Your beliefs are unique and your world is filtered through them. When they *feel* true, they seem to be.

If you believe you are in danger, your mind and body, even your gene expression, will change instantly. Your beliefs will alert your immune system demanding adrenaline and cortisol to materialize into molecules of action, even when the danger is imagined. If you believe you are safe, your body will act accordingly. Your beliefs are a map that is shaped by reality, and that rewrite reality as you believe it.

In your body, a belief can turn a sugar pill into a cure that actually works, calling upon the power of placebo to heal you. If you are in total touch with your body's needs for exercise, water, healthy food, and a clean environment, you won't need to believe in diets or training programs. Tune your beliefs to the needs and necessities of existence in the same way a bird builds a nest and rest in it.

Beliefs are the monuments of your reality. This includes your beliefs about the world, yourself, what everything is worth, and if it's possible. Beliefs can be built with any combination of facts, logical proof, emotional proof, pure fantasy, and empirical experiences. Explore the art and refine your architecture.

Your beliefs are the bridge over which your visions cross into actions.

A belief allows you to create a reality known only to you, including what you see, hear, and experience. The very core nature of a belief is to seem undeniably real and thus no two realities are the same. Yet when people share a belief, they often call it a truth. Understand this and every other creature is understandable.

A belief can travel through space and time in the form of an idea. It can build nations, topple tyrants, and inspire people to dance in new ways. The seeds of beliefs can be as small as that thought in the back of your mind. This is where faith comes in handy, allowing you to choose to believe in what you would like to have happen next. In the garden of your life grow the fruits of your beliefs, and sometimes you may need to zoom out, to see them.

Essence

“ *Your beliefs and reality create each other.* **”**

Sidestep Your Beliefs

Think of something you believe is true, you disbelieve, or you are unsure about.

Ask, "What if it *isn't* so?"

Ask, "What if it *is* so?"

Explore What It Is to "Know"

A human truth is, by definition, a human belief. How do you believe you can tell the difference between what you believe you know and what you know you believe?

Who Is the Boss?

Sometimes simple questions reveal the nature of your beliefs:

- Think of a belief you hold.
- If you didn't hold this belief, what would happen?
- How will you know if this belief isn't true?
- What does this belief allow you to do, think, and feel?

For example, if you have a habit you feel you cannot change, ask yourself what belief you are holding for this habit to be useful. Look for a belief that allows the habit to change while preserving the same goal.

Try a Different Lens

Try filtering the world through a belief that it is a wonderful magical place full of absurd humor where everything happens for a reason.

Maybe Logic

Instead of debating beliefs that cannot be proven, rate both the probability that it is true, and that it isn't, from 0 percent to 100 percent.

"I believe in ghosts to 30 percent because _____."

And at the same time

"I don't believe in ghosts to 50 percent, because _____."

This is a version of "maybe logic" and is a useful way of herding beliefs.

This version builds on the ideas originally presented by Robert Anton Wilson in The Lives and Ideas of Robert Anton Wilson

Explore a Belief

Is this belief one you

- choose to believe?
- can't help believing?
- think you believe?
- feel you believe?
- cannot make yourself believe?

To contain water, you need something other than water.

~ Don T. Bidoux

MEMORIES OF YOU

It's never too late to have a happy childhood.

~ Ben Furman

The world you see in front of you would cease to exist as soon as you close your eyes if you couldn't remember it. Without your memories you are eternally now in a spotless mind where every impression is new. In fact, your whole idea of the world is created with artifacts from your vast river of memories. The sound of somebody biting an apple, the texture of wood, and looking into the sun on a bright day. Memories offer your mind references to analyze the past, understand the now, and imagine the future. They are placeholders for your self-image. Memories are the magic of the past recreated in the now. They are the basis of what you believe you know.

Imagine trying to find out who you are if there were no memories of your past. Your memories are the tour guides and map of who you are and why you are here. Invite an artist to paint some of the most inspiring ones in magnificent ways. Ask them to paint some you would like to have in the future while they are at it.

As soon as you close your eyes or go inside your thoughts, you enter the theater of your mind where memories are recreated by your imagination. On this stage, memories can grow wild, be planted on purpose and weeded. They can be diluted by creating multiple versions. They can be transformed by changing the perspective from which you look at them. They can be enlarged, pushed aside, and summoned out of nowhere, bringing insights long overdue or just in time.

Every time you send your salmons of attention upstream to fetch a memory it will be recreated as a copy of the original, and not an exact one. It may even be different every time you fetch it. Once you have thought about it, you restore it, saving the copy as a new original. Part of you paints this canvas every time, and if you get to know the artist, you can cross the border between memories and imagination, and create the memories that serve you best. This can be wonderfully confusing, since the thin line between memories and imagination is that of the chicken and the egg. You can imagine a version of your childhood you would love to have had, and benefit from it as it happens.

If your mind were a cinema there would be a screen. Some memories are experienced as if you are on the screen being a part of the movie, and in others you might be sitting at a comfortable distance, maybe even with a remote control in your hand that can replay episodes and pause them. Put on your director's hat and sunglasses, lean back, and look at your life up to now as an exciting adventure about to evolve into the most exciting and memorable part of the story. Ask what you need to learn from the past for a great next episode.

Essence

" *The story you tell about yourself can be told in many different ways.* **"**

Explorations

Dilute your memories: When food is too salty, you can add more of everything except salt until it becomes tasty. When your mind has more than one version of a memory, it dilutes whatever spice that may annoy you. Make as many as necessary.

Edit your memories: Summon a memory and explore the sensory fabric it is made of, then use your imagination to change any part of that fabric: enlarge, diminish, refocus, brighten, dampen, soften it, or explore moving it to a different location in the physical space of your mind.

Point your view: Remember something through the eyes of the other person, or through the eyes of a fly passing by.

Draw like a kid: Imagine a memory for which you want to change the emotional response. Draw the situation with your nondominant hand, like stick figures.

Rewrite the past: Imagine a past experience both as you remember it and how you would like it to have played out instead.

Trust your memories for what they are: Even if a camera had recorded every step and moment of your life up to this moment and you look at that film, your state of mind will still affect what you remember and how you remember it.

Create memory snacks: A memory can activate great emotions and physical reactions. Stack them up, call for them when needed, keep your best ones at the top of the box. Have photos of your loved ones in your wallet.

To Remember, First Forget!

If you forget something, you will have a harder time remembering it the more you try. If you change the subject completely, your subconscious usually brings it back. If you forgot something entering a room, try walking out and back in.

Reflect

Your memories of procedures and skills like walking, reading, cooking, and swimming are stored in both mind and muscle memory, so if you lost the memories you would still be able to use the skills, and you would have no idea why; if you forget that you went to school, you will still be able to read.

The rain interacts with your existence without understanding it, and so can you.

~ Don T. Bidoux

CURSE OR BLESSING

I don't want credibility; I want incredibility.

~ mentioned by Timothy Leary, psychonaut

In the grand puzzle everything fits perfectly somewhere. Some people can hear and see things others can't. Historically many have been regarded as people with extraordinary abilities. Should humanity discover a medical herb that heals every melancholy, frustration, and depression, we could wake up to find a vast body of human expression has evaporated. Should the cure include every eccentric ability, we could lose our scientists, artists, painters, poets, visionaries, and oracles.

Sometimes there is meaning in moaning.

If we can accept the idea that any human behavior is an attempt to adapt to a circumstance, to survive or thrive in a specific situation, then it will seem natural that when it works, we call it "grit" and when it annoys we call it "disorder." In fact, the frame we hang around it is a cultural and societal lens.

When a characteristic distinguishes somebody as an individual, we admiringly call it a personality trait. Be that trait a problem for the person or somebody around them, they might choose to view it as a disorder. If there is a personality trait not yet blooming to its full flourish, we might think of it as a trait to be developed.

Fire is a problem if it swallows a house; kept in a fireplace, it can be both useful and romantic. An attention span that stops a young person from diving into a concentrated effort can make them the single individual who spots that fire before it spreads.

The psychological ability to focus intensely on a narrow range of interests to an extreme depth at the cost of social interaction allows those who have it to spend thousands of hours developing unimaginable skills. When you add a chimney to a fireplace you can enjoy it without the smoke bothering you.

If a society produces a large number of people with any form of syndrome, then maybe that is a signal about the society, not about the symptoms.

Entertaining an owl is usually best done at night and in a tree, any other circumstance may cause distress. If you are pressing cubes into round holes, take a step back and wonder why. Every flower will grow in the right circumstances; every spice is a flavor out of context. If your eyesight is less than great you might get glasses, but you don't change your title. Any ability, no matter how strange, is considered normal once enough people develop it.

You have an ocean of possible abilities for your experiences and circumstances to bring forth. Define them not as a curse or a blessing; explore how, where, when, and with whom they can be useful.

Essence

❝*Find the blessing in every ability.*❞

Explore

1. Look at the story of your life as the journey of a hero where the future is still to be told.

2. What are your current abilities that may be useful?

3. If there is an ability that seems less useful up to now, imagine an absurd situation where that specific ability may be what makes a difference.

4. What other abilities would you like to have to make your journey fulfilling?

Reflect

A mental disorder is a syndrome characterized by clinically significant disturbance in an individual's cognition, emotion regulation, or behavior that reflects a dysfunction in the psychological, biological, or developmental processes underlying mental functioning. Mental disorders are usually associated with significant distress in social, occupational, or other important activities. An expectable or culturally approved response to a common stressor or loss, such as the death of a loved one, is not a mental disorder. Socially deviant behavior (e.g., political, religious, or sexual) and conflicts that are primarily between the individual and society are not mental disorders unless the deviance or conflict results from a dysfunction in the individual, as described above."

~ Introduction to the *Diagnostic and Statistical Manual of Mental Disorders*

Everything is simple. It is people who complicate things.

~ Albert Camus

BOTTOM LINE:
THE MENU IS NOT THE MEAL

Even when you believe you know the rules and circumstances, you know there is more to it. There is more to you.

Let's all make beliefs: Your beliefs and reality create each other.

Memories of you: The story you tell about yourself can be told in many different ways.

Curse or blessing: Find the blessing in every ability.

UNDER THE HOOD

Your state of mind adapts. Water will flow around any object placed in its path.

Your sovereign states and
the thrill of a skill
allow you to feel it baby,
because when you
find your groove
you can Lead your zeppelin.

YOUR SOVEREIGN STATES

A truth may set you free, but will it make you laugh?

~ Don T. Bidoux

Water will seek to flow around any object placed in its path and, like that river, your state is your capacity in a given moment. Forgetting what you believe you are capable of can liberate superpowers.

When you are in a state of hunger your focus is on what can be eaten; in a state of restlessness, you look for something to do. Your focus will change your state, will change your focus. As this information flows through your mind, notice what happens next.

Your state is the door that can open up for your best self to step through, a straight line between your abilities and your performance. If a cloud of doubt shadows your self-esteem or skills, you shall literally sun dance, because any shift in your physiology will shift your state. Breathe deeply into the rhythms of relaxation and notice how your posture follows. Let your shoulders relax and embrace the pull of gravitation.

And as you do, move your attention to your attention, for the voice and images your attention creates in your head are the chickens or the eggs that rule the state you are moving into right now. Guide them to desirable images in the part of your mind that listens to them. Build a museum of artwork that inspires your subconscious to straighten your posture and invite the corners of your mouth to those of your eyes.

Where your mind and your body meet, there is a campfire of emotions, oracles of your actions. They will allow you to predict the probability of what you will feel. In the footsteps of every life experience, you will find a saved program of actions should a similar experience linger into the radar of your subconscious senses.

Anything that reaches your senses will thus play the harp of your previously tuned desires to move toward or away from these signals: the sound of boiling water, a hand on the shoulder confirming a shared emotion, the smell of burning wood, a peculiar color of the setting sun.

Dolphins can be trained with sardines, and we can too. If you condition the states you like to find yourself in, you can step into peak performance with the snap of a finger.

No you is an island entire of itself; every you is a piece of the continent, a part of the main; a main with four basic elements in action, that of a perceived situation, an environment in which it plays out, the company of others or lack thereof and ultimately that etheric perspective through which we swim our existence. The river of time.

While the harp of your senses is tuned to the needs of the mammal hosting you, it will vibrate in resonance with the energy of every living being around you. The tuning forks are the neural mirrors so helpful in allowing you to detect the moods and states surrounding you. The three basic states of your being are tuned to embrace joy and play, avoid pain, or simply survive without interference from your marvelous brain.

The multiple layers and dimensions of your physical, emotional, and mental capacities are summoned into a state that seems to answer the call of every moment.

Essence

**Your constantly shifting states are a liquid portal to your capacities.**

Explore the Grammar of Your Physiology

Every part of your current state is connected to your physiology. Be it your breathing, pulse, sweating, stiffness, balance, tension, adrenaline, eyelids … there is no shift in your physiology without a shift in thoughts and emotions, however subtle it may be. And, the other way around.

To shift your state, shift your body:

1. Breathe in deeply and hold for a few seconds, and notice what happens to your posture and sense of control. Breathe out with the posture maintained.

2. Relax your muscles to land in the moment with the full weight of your being.

3. Put an amused smile, however undetectable, on your lips and allow that same amusement to shape the corners of your eyes.

4. Imagine a great song, music that makes you want to dance. Imagine that it is playing in your heart. Vibrating into your arms and legs.

5. BONUS: Shift your temperature, for example, by splashing cold water in your face. It will trigger a reflex in your nervous system that lowers your heart rate.

Explore Peripheral Vision

When you are acting under pressure you will auto-activate "tunnel vision" to focus on what you need to resolve. This will suspend the playfulness of your creative mind. The opposite of tunnel vision is when you blur your focus with your eyes open and "stare dreamily into space," which changes your state and opens you up to lateral thoughts.

1. Change posture. If you are sitting, stand; if you are standing, sit.
2. Hands out in front of you, palms up.
3. Breathe in, hold your breath, and let your eyes gaze peripherally into space.
4. Find a mild and slightly crazy smile.
5. Allow your fingers to play a piano, upside down.
6. Breathe out and see how much gravity your body can embrace.
7. Notice what is different.

Anchor a State

1. Think of a state you would like to be in by design.
2. Notice the grammar of your physiology in this state: your breathing, posture, tension, point of gravity, fluidity of movements.

3. Notice what your mind focuses on. What is the image? What is your internal dialogue?

4. Remember a situation where you felt this way, and what you may have looked like to somebody else.

5. Step into this memory of yourself, enhance and notice every part of the sensations involved, the energy itself. Make sure your eyes and smile join in.

6. Clench a fist hard and let go, fast. This is your anchor to activate this state in the future.

Change Pants, Change State

Do your gardening in your best pants: dress for the occasion, or dress the opposite, either way it will change how you approach and feel about it.

Tango Somebody into Your Perspective

When somebody is agitated or frustrated, in a state of not having their needs met, you cannot ask them to calm down. That is the same as rejecting their feelings. See their energy as an invitation to dance, and join them at their level, then make an unexpected yet subtle move into something else: "Yes, I agree that you [use their words, for example "think I am a pumpernickel"] and now let's find the ice cream."

Review Your Avatars

In a model of personality psychology, you are assumed to have a number of basic avatar states that you activate depending on context and intention: a lover, a warrior, an inner child, a playful puppy.

If this is so, is there anything you would like to know or change about them?

The word is not the thing

~ Alfred Korzybski, General Semantics,
the critical use of words and other symbols

THE THRILL OF A SKILL

Tap into the rest of the ocean.

~ Don T. Bidoux

You may be walking a road often traveled, or be performing a skill that no longer requires the attention of your mind, leaving it free to wander to other places. And as you do, time seems to fly, after which you may find yourself surprised that you have come to completion, just vaguely remembering the details, with a timeless sense of satisfaction.

The art of mindless actions is a flow of the being you are, and one of the most blissful states to visit. It grows from a skill of any kind, performed beyond consciousness. And, you may wonder, what a gardener brings to the flower of skills.

A kiss can be discovered by a novice, requiring but a curious and playful attitude, the willingness to explore and embrace every step, even the stumbles. Naught is required in the ways of resources except the very lips in question, and those of the other. 'Tis not like archery, where a bow and arrow are required to fulfill the perfection of the skill.

You may have heard of a kiss, and many a story might guide you, but none of them will surpass the exceptional learning delivered by your personal experience. Given time, and enough lips, you can evolve into an acrobat of emotional devotion.

Imagine every possible talent you have the potential to potentiate, still not uncovered. Prime yourself with tools, tricks and tenacity to curiously unveil them, and you will create an amusement park for life to enjoy.

Most of us have talents we are unaware of. Some of these precious pearls can only be recognized from the outside, by others. A talent can be cultivated into a skill; it is a potential that will manifest in the presence of practice, devotion, and playfulness.

Essence

66 *The mother of extraordinary skills is obsessive, compulsive practice.* **99**

Explore the Duck

People shipwrecked on tropical islands sometimes draw faces on coconuts and talk to them to maintain sanity. In problem solving, there is a phenomenon called rubber ducking, in which you explain your problem to a rubber duck out loud and the answers will appear within you. Trust the duck.

Explore the talent of timing

A band leader once said about a musician by the name of Charlie Parker, "He's the sax player with the best timing in the world, but let's get somebody who shows up for the gig."

Be the Sun Mirror

Make the other person feel fully seen and heard by looking directly at them and allowing them to speak. Be curious about them and feed their own words back so they know you heard what they actually said. If they say, "I'm having *one of those days*," you can say something as simple as, "*One of those days*, huh?" Smile like a sun, as if they are your friend, even if they are.

Explore Speed-Reading

Try going from focusing on a letter on this page, then a word, then a sentence. Continue to making the whole page blurry. Notice what happens. Speed-reading builds on the ability to scan pages at a time instead of single words.

Dark Sight

When you get out of bed at night, your eyes will adapt to night vision. If you turn on the lights you will adjust to brighter ambience and lose this night vision. You can keep your night vision in one eye by closing the other eye before turning on a brighter light and keeping the first one closed until the light is turned off.

Talent Beyond Genes

Even if thousands of hours can lead to mastery, you can develop a higher than average and quite impressive level of skill in almost any area in just a couple of days.

1. Find somebody who is really good at something.
2. Study every detail of what they seem to do.
3. Close your eyes and visualize them in your mind doing what they are good at.
4. In your mind, see yourself stepping into their bodies, and doing what they are good at.
5. Now test this in real life, just a few times.
6. Do something completely different, shake it off.
7. Practice again, embrace your improvements.
8. Repeat the whole procedure again until you have integrated their skill into yours.

Tune into your flow

One of the happiest states you can be in is the state of flow, where time is suspended, and you are using a skill without conscious thought at a high level of achievement. By understanding the mechanics of flow you can prepare for awesomeness in the same way a surfer does, being able to recognize the perfect wave before it comes, and be ready to ride it once it arrives.

- To perform in flow, you need to develop a skill.
- To find your flow, you need to use that skill at an appropriate level of challenge.
- To stay in your flow, let go of critical thinking and self-consciousness.
- If you are not thinking and doing this and it is pleasant, you are in flow.

Flow can take your mind off anything that bothers you. It can be summoned with any type of game or activity. What activities allow you to relax and lose track of time?

Dear God, can I have some more time?
I have things to do.

~ Don T. Bidoux

FEEL IT, BABY

Our lack of respect for the balance of things that we don't understand is amazing.

~ Don T. Bidoux

A poet once said that your actions are singing the needs of your body, your mind, your genes, and your soul. When they are in tune, they will direct your attention and efforts safely to that which can bring joy, pleasure, and meaning to your existence.

They make us move mountains, cross oceans, and bring nations to war. They can set siblings against each other and bring peace in chaos. The dialogue between your soul, the needs of your body, and how your mind interprets the requests of society, will bring spice to your brew of emotions.

While you have them and create them, you may not be able to interpret them at all times, since they pull their information not only from your conscious rational mind, but also from the vastness of your subliminal life experience, and what it seems to mean to you. Hence, they may create theatrical performances in your sleeping and waking mind, be it dreams of different kinds.

In this dialogue between your true needs and what you believe will meet them, there will be plenty of room for interpretation, and with so many contributing parts, what you feel is never the truth nor a lie. It just seems so when you feel it.

From an evolutionary point of view, there is a neurology and advantage to every emotional response. Anger can be of great use in the face of injustice, at the final run of a marathon, or if you're opening the stuck lid on a jar of honey. Fear is valuable when taking precautions against a possible danger. What seems like a depression in a mind, can be a body that needs to rest and rejuvenate. Every emotion has a positive intention, also the darker ones.

The guidelines to your emotions come from the culture you are swimming in, from your life experience, the feelings in your gut. This explains how differently two people can react to what seem to be the same stimuli, since their lives are as unique as drops of water. Ask not what life makes you feel; ask what your feeling, wishes you to do about life.

The biggest obstacle to life is fear. A lion tamer walks into the cage with confidence because they have learned how to handle the situation. To feel confident letting fear go, embrace it and ask what it wants you to learn.

Embrace the possible discomfort of confusion. It is a sign that you are presented with information unknown to you, a sign of new possibilities. When you are confused, you are entering the portal of moreness.

Emotions are information. This information can be traced back to your mind. When you feel something, what do you need to believe in order to feel that? Then ask if what you believe is true, and what will happen if it isn't so.

Your emotional responses are hardwired to your physiology. You can get "cold chills down your spine" or "heartache" or "butterflies in your stomach." When you shift an emotion your body language will change. Therefore, when you are stuck in an emotional response, changing your physiology can shift the emotion. Cold water in your face will calm your heart.

Embrace every emotion and ask what it needs to have happen next.

Essence

“ *An emotion is a dialogue between all of your dimensions and needs. Listen closely.* ”

Explore if It Is

As you encounter an emotion seeming to tell you something, ask:

"What if it is, so?"

"What if it isn't, so?"

When in Doubt; Act!

If you are not sure about doing, or not doing, do. The emotion you feel after is a confirmation, while the one before is a prediction. Nothing is forever, and a lot can be undone.

Sculpting Emotional Responses

When you experience emotions that you would like to change you can use your body to create a state that opens a door to a preferred set of emotions:

- Put your palms together, rub them in a circular motion, as if you are rolling a glass pearl between them. You don't want to crush it and you don't want to drop it. Continue doing this during this whole exercise.

- Hum a tune gently under your breath for a minute, any nursery rhyme will do.

- While continuing the movement of your palms, look for a memory of a situation that reminds you of an emotion you would like to have. Sense the difference, however small or large it may be. Where it is in your body. What it feels like. How you breathe.

- Continue the movement of your palms a minute or two and hum the tune again. Then stop and notice what is different.

This is a simple form of a technique called Havening, of which there are many other variants for sculpting neural responses as described in the book *When the Past is Always Present* by Ronald A. Ruden (Routledge Taylor and Francis Group 2011).

If it feels good, it probably feels good.

~ Don T. Bidoux

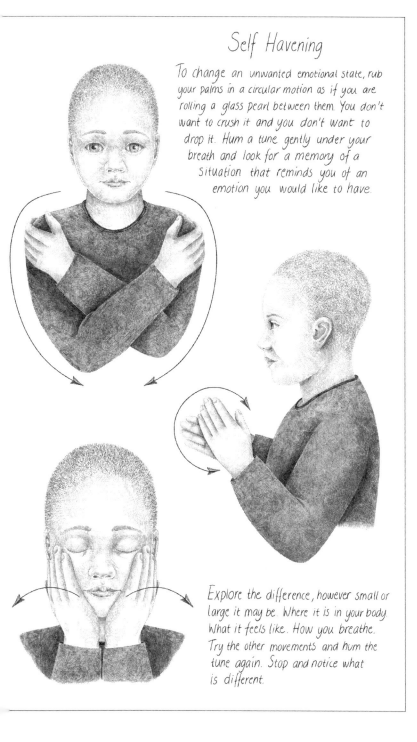

Self Havening

To change an unwanted emotional state, rub your palms in a circular motion as if you are rolling a glass pearl between them. You don't want to crush it and you don't want to drop it. Hum a tune gently under your breath and look for a memory of a situation that reminds you of an emotion you would like to have.

Explore the difference, however small or large it may be. Where it is in your body. What it feels like. How you breathe. Try the other movements and hum the tune again. Stop and notice what is different.

FIND YOUR GROOVE

Without music, life would be a mistake.

~ Friedrich Nietzsche

The earth you are flying on right now creates a low frequency wave of sound, resonating with the surrounding ionosphere at the rhythm of your meditative brain waves in the ocean of your mind.

Your heart has an individual groove to it, a fingerprint of your organism pulsating in reaction to conditions within and around you. Music is one of your most basic needs. It has followed you from the first chant, dance, and drumming of your ancestral cave mother, and permeates every part of society. Humans have marched into war with it, worked to it, mourned with it, and used it to set the mood for love. Music is a state-changer, peacemaker, and opener of minds.

Music can be a part of your identity. Just like food, music can be nutrition for the soul, an energy infusion or an emotional accessory. It can lift you up, before you go-go.

Music is a campfire of sound to gather around. As the warmth of the music spreads, bodies may start to move subtly, or energetically, a notion to enjoy a shared motion. When performed live, there is a magical component reminding us of the here and now, of being alive and capable of sharing.

When the challenges of life overwhelm us, some of us will gradually disengage with these uncomfortable emotions, creating a silent bubble out of rhythm with the world. Your heart rate, breathing, digestive system, and thought patterns may stray into a mist of disconnection, and by engaging in music, rhythm, and harmonies can bring order to the chaos of dissonance. If you water the flowers of your moods with the sunshine of a great groove, your neural roots will rearrange.

Your taste in music holds a message about your personality and past experiences. When you tune in and dance to a new type of music, your personality evolves.

Essence

“ *Explore your soundtrack. Push up the volume. Dance outside your box.* ”

Explore Your Soundtrack

1. Listen to your life right now, your groove.

2. If you had a soundtrack, what would it be?

3. Turn it on and move to it.

4. Try another one, explore what happens

Explore Flock Breathing and Timing

When humans flock together and synchronize our breathing there is a calming effect, a connection. This is what happens when we sing the same song in a choir, march to our defenses, or lay down a railroad track with a work song. Rhythmical breathing aligns your energy. Singing is tactical breathing. Try it.

We are the songs you learn to sing ... We're here to make you feel alive.

~ Lyrics by The Soundtrack of Our Lives, Swedish rock band

LEAD YOUR ZEPPELIN

I don't do regrets.

~ Lemmy Kilmister, legendary singer and bass
player in Motörhead

As your adventure evolves, many days will be like others and then suddenly it changes. When you arrive at what seems to be the end of a rope, there is a part of your mind and heart that can change everything. Like money and guitars, you can inherit it, earn it, borrow it from others, and it doesn't necessarily qualify you to play it. It can be printed on a metaphorical T-shirt and understood in a glance.

Daring to live can be as simple as accepting the fact that death is inevitable. Without it no life. Without life no frailty, and with nothing to lose, no value. As you face your challenges, remind yourself that there is only one person responsible for your wellbeing, happiness, and pursuits in life. This person grows as you do. Life defines your challenges. Your attitude defines how you handle them.

Your life experiences and what you choose to believe and value define your attitudes.

Each game changer will allow a new part of you to evolve. It can be the arrival of children, fortune or poverty, a job, a relationship, a loved one, a change of physical health. In the process of integrating a new dimension of yourself, a change in your field of values and identity may arise. From this you need to emerge with new norms that allow you to perform, to be the new you.

If you truly want to accept and embrace the frailty, uncertainty, and possible total connection of life then take a step forward. Don't limit yourself to being a rebel, lover, perfectionist, fighter, helper, poet, a hippie, or a philosopher. Be all at least once and more.

Had your parents kept chewing your food, your teeth might never have grown. Sometimes we do the same raising our inner child. Anytime you find yourself explaining why you're not doing what you want in life by pointing at time, money, age, or any other circumstance, you may be missing the point: It's not why you believe you can't, it's why you don't.

Your attitude shifts everything; it is the menu in your choices of handling life. Like a stoic in ancient Greece, you can skip a meal to explore being hungry, preparing yourself to smile in the face of temporary starvation. Look for the attitudes that allow you to live in a way that you will talk fondly about around the campfires of the future.

Dare to be mediocre, dare to be enough, dare to be brilliant, and dare to dazzle the world. To love deeply, dare to be hurt. To win, dare losing everything you have fought for. Dare to be scared and vulnerable and depressed. Dare to rise from the ashes and shine.

Essence

66 *When the game changes, find the
attitude that changes
the game.* 99

Explore Pragmatic Optimism

1. Change what can be changed

2. Leave the rest

3. Look for meaning

4. Engage with others

5. Look for a future use in what is happening now.

Practice Stoicism

- Imagine the worst, then aim for the best.

- Force a smile. It shows your body the way.

- Skip a meal and explore hunger.

- Screw up, forgive yourself, learn, and move on.

Explore Castanedaism

The Toltec approach from the character Juan Castaneda by Don Miguel Ruiz suggests four simple principles to live by when interacting with others, called *The Four Agreements*, with two do's and two don'ts.

1. Be Impeccable With Your Word
   - Take full responsibility for the effects of your words.

2. Don't Take Anything Personally
   - What others say and do is a projection of their reality.

3. Don't Make Assumptions
   - Your thoughts and beliefs are unique to you. Maybe to anybody else.

4. Always Do Your Best
   - Once you have done the best you are capable of in any given circumstance, you can do no more. Make sure to Satisfice what is best, and why.

Death is frightening, and so is Eternal Life.

~ Mason Cooley, witty American aphorist

BOTTOM LINE:
UNDER THE HOOD

Your sovereign states: Your constantly shifting states are a liquid portal to your capacities

The thrill of a skill: The mother of extraordinary skills is obsessive, compulsive practice.

Feel it, baby: An emotion is a dialogue between all of your dimensions and needs. Listen closely.

Find your groove. Explore your soundtrack. Push up the volume. Dance outside your box.

Lead your zeppelin: When the game changes, find the attitude that changes the game.

Rules will be broken. Friendships will be tested. And huge risks will be taken. But they're small prices to pay for true love and freedom, right?

~ Words, by Lisi Harrison, *Monster High*

THY WILL BE DONE

I n some cases, it may seem obvious why you do what you do; in others less so.

May the source be with you and
your bucket of resilience, because
beyond reason, you can
train your tiger and optimize your
cruise control, as you
prime your Optimus,
riding the pony of love
with your chain of tools.
And as you do...

MAY THE SOURCE BE WITH YOU

Every change in a living organism starts with a
positive intention of some kind. This intention may
not be clear to anybody, even to the organism itself.

~ Don T. Bidoux

The river of your intentions flows from many sources. Your body will signal for rest and rejuvenation; your senses may let you know if there is a fly on your nose or a pleasure attainable even before you become consciously aware of it. Your genes will wish for you to mate and reproduce your uniqueness, causing attraction to stir. Your mind and something beyond it will seek to connect, to create order and find meaning, to be seen and contribute. To find pleasure, excitement, and to express yourself. To grow.

When you find yourself acting out a thought, feeling, or behavior, it has come from somewhere, on an errand of some kind. There is no emotion or sensation without a source. Follow that river upstream and look for its origin, the message it is looking to deliver, even if the message itself seems out of place.

The wonderful construction of your senses can come to conclusions that may appear as a mere tingling in your gut, and when you train yourself to listen you will intuitively intuit. You can know without knowing how and allow your intellect to sort out the science if possible.

A suppressed urge or craving outside your awareness can cause you to initiate a series of actions that may seem coincidental. This is where you may wish to notice the difference between what you seem to want and what you actually need.

To connect is a fundamental human need. We are creatures of flock and hardwired to be a part of something, anything, in some way, in any way. You can be connected through a belief, habit, or interest over time and space. Through a bloodline or a shared experience. You can connect to a flock such as your family, your ancestors, your countrymen; to those who like the same art or causes. You can be connected to nature, to animals, or to an idea. This connection provides a sense of belonging, to be seen and acknowledged, to know that you are.

When you say you like surprises, you probably mean surprises you like. This is part of your relationship with order and predictability. Predictability can make you feel comfortable, safe, and in control, or it can become boring. Disorder can be exciting and inviting you to step out of your comfort zone. And it can be frustrating. The art of finding balance between chaos and control seems to be what creates a sense of magic in your life.

Significance is the mysterious core of every existential question, the meaning of things, and is but a matter of perspective, a social lens through which we regard ourselves and others. To feel special, unique, wanted, necessary, or useful in a certain context helps us collaborate and create societies where we tend to seek the company of those who provide us with this feeling. The roots of connection, significance, and order are sometimes inseparable and at times seemingly apart.

Whatever emotions and thoughts you find less than pleasurable, at times maybe even tormenting, instead of suppressing, numbing, or trying to escape them, look for the usefulness that allowed them to evolve over millions of years. Through this lens every emotion may hold the answer to a question you didn't ask yet.

Any action by a living being can only be fully understood from the perspective of the unique journey of that being. What they believe they know will make them believe they value the actions they take, and so will you.

Essence

"Each body thinks, feels, and does everything for a reason. Look for it."

Explore the Source of Actions

1. Observe a behavior in yourself or another being.

2. Assume the behavior is looking to solve something.

3. Ask what must be valued, over other options, to initiate this action.

4. Ask what must be believed for this value to be true.

5. Ask how this belief came to be.

6. Explore a belief that may promote a different behavior.

Explore the Options

1. Do the exercise above.

2. Ask if any other action or behavior can meet the same need.

Explore Feeding Demons

In the book *Feeding Your Demons,* author Tsultrim Allione describes the practice of the sensational eleventh-century, female Buddhist monk, Machig Labdrön, of approaching the source of your inner demons. Instead of fighting demons, listen to them. Ask not what they demand or want, find out what they need and feed them that.

A simplified version of the method is this.

1. Close your eyes. Allow yourself to be playfully creative and envision your demon. What does it look like, specifically?

2. Ask what it seems to "want" or "demand" of you. The drinking demon to drink, the anxiety demon to fear, the hoarding demon to collect, the perfection demon to be impeccable.

3. Now imagine moving over into the demon and answer what it "needs" or hopes to gain by getting what it demands. A smoking demon may be trying to calm you down and a drinking demon to relax and take your mind off something else.

4. Float back into yourself and imagine surrendering completely what the demon needs, by giving it full calmness or relaxation or attention or love.

5. Just sit for a while and then explore what the demon seems to be like now.

You want to be loved; failing that, admired; failing that, feared; failing that, hated and despised. You want to evoke some sort of sentiment. Your soul shudders before oblivion and seeks connection at any price.

~ Hjalmar Söderberg from *Doctor Glas*, the story of a physician who deals with love and moral issues

YOUR BUCKET
OF RESILIENCE

*Do not judge me by my success, judge me by how
many times I fell down and got back up again.*

~ Never proven to be said by Nelson Mandela,
but in his spirit

A bucket will fill up with water at the speed of the rain
falling into it. Should there be a tap at the bottom to
regulate the levels, it will never need to overflow.

Every piece of information that sails like a drop of rain into
the senses of your body will be collected in the bucket that
empties itself to make room for new information while it
looks to create responses and reactions for similar situations
in the future.

How you perceive information, even beyond your consciousness, is tied to one of the three states that rule your
responses.

When you engage in an action from your state of playfulness, of light and love, you are joyfully exploring something desirable. A concert of energy will run through your system accompanied by a higher heart rate and excitement. Children are intuitive masters at doing this for hours and hours until they switch off and recover by closing down into a deep sleep during which buckets are emptied to make room for more of the same the next day.

Should a warning flag be raised that there may be a threat to your emotional or physical dimensions, you will shift into a state of defense. Your playfulness will diminish and, depending on what happens next, spiral into scanning your reality through the lens of what to avoid. This spiral can accelerate into a focused trance where priorities are radically changed, and pleasantry will step aside to maintain safety. Now the bucket is filling up faster than it empties, which will lead to the release of action chemicals like adrenaline and cortisol into your blood and changes in priorities from digesting food to pumping more oxygen into your brain.

Your mind plays an important role in the maintenance of your bucket. Every word you allow it to form that paints an image of something playfully desirable will open a tap at the bottom allowing the levels of stress to stay low, giving you access to your full range of actions and thoughts. You can improve your ability to notice your levels of resilience by learning the simple signs of raised defenses: when your laughter has gone silent because your humor is asleep, and you are more focused on solving things than on enjoying doing so. In times of trouble, fake a smile and trim your sails until it feels natural.

There seems to be three main approaches to the games of life: you can play for fun, you can play to avoid danger, and you can play to survive. If you play the zones of defense and survival for long, the importance of ingeniously letting out the steam increases and can be learned. When your sleeping patterns tell you there seems to be a disturbance in the force, take a step back and look at the full picture. What can you change and what can't you? Let go of what you can't and change what you can. Nobody has worried themselves out of a situation. Your actions shall set you free.

When your bucket is full, you will move through a chain of reactions designed by evolution. At first you will freeze, to become invisible and to scan for more information. Eventually your safety system will flip into an extraordinary survival state in which your intellect, rational thought, and emotional needs will stand back for the instincts that have kept you alive since you were related to reptiles; finding safety, fighting back, or playing dead.

Keep an eye on your bucket, and when something rocks your boat, sit down, center yourself, take the oars, and look for balance. Trim what can be trimmed, step back, and look at the whole. Tap into the resilience of a flock if you can find one. Rest, recover, and bring yourself to the now. Look for the meaning beyond the meaning and a smile that shows the way.

Essence

❝ *To shift smoothly between survival, defense, and playfulness, cultivate your resilience.* ❞

Explore the Standards

While it may seem impossible to let go of a bad thought, it is easier to embrace a different thought, especially in a flow. Try exercising in a flow that requires you to do nothing but that. Seek active relaxation in socializing or reading. Move your body, breathe deeply, walk in slow motion. Take care of your body like a mother who cares for her child more than anything. Brush your teeth twice, once with toothpaste and once more with love. Sleep as much as your system will allow. Seek the company of nature.

Prepare for the worst, hope for the best, and give it your maximum possible effort!

~ A proverb from the Stoic thinkers of 300 BCE who believed that a happy life involves the cultivation of great mental states.

BEYOND REASON

Like a Danish pastry, your understanding of life
affects the width more than the length.

~ Don T. Bidoux

Your life unfolds as it happens, right now, and everything that appears on the radar of your senses, be it conscious or not, will prompt you to make a decision of some kind. To say hello to somebody, to choose what to eat, to ask for directions, or to allow a situation to unfold.

To help you make these decisions, small or large, fast or slow, intuitive or rational; there is a repertoire of tools vividly supported by your imagination, a canvas of senses that will allow you to create alternative scenarios, compare them to previous experiences, facts, pros, cons, ideas, and feel them out as if they were enacted, before you choose, often at a speed beyond imagination, and without even surfacing as a rational thought in the theater of your conscious mind.

Greek philosophers suggested the metaphor of a chariot pulled by two horses in this theater of the mind: the horse of passion and the horse of reason. If only one horse runs, your chariot will go in circles. If they pull in opposite directions your chariot will linger at best. The chariot is run by habits most of the time, guided by impulses created from past experiences and dreams about where it should be heading. When something unexpected comes in the way of this chariot, there will be a vote between all involved parts for a decision that seems appropriate.

In the crystal ball of your universe, many dimensions come into play when the future is to be told. And like a fish in a river there are ways for you to align the forces that push and pull you into actions. The conscious tip of this dynamic iceberg rests on multiple processes underneath.

Rational thinking is a myriad of systems that align facts with experiences, hopes, and fears while looking for confirmation in a feeling from the gut or the heart. It is a collaboration of emotional rationalization in the nation of you.

Your rational system is curious, eager to find answers by looking for patterns, and investigating possible causes, effects, and correlations. It strives to create a narrative, the story of "you" and "the world" so that it can plan how this story may evolve, and it is, by nature, often one step behind your intuition.

As your system sums up everything it can into senses; into sounds, images, tastes, and sensations of the past, it creates a theater of possible scenarios and "feelings" about what your next actions can be.

This became evident through a man by the name of Elliot. This man was successful in the world of monetary transactions, running a small empire. One day his head started hurting. It turned out to be a tumor, and through an operation the tumor was successfully removed leaving all his intellectual abilities intact. Or so it seemed, but one small connection had been lost: the one that allows rational decisions to be confirmed by emotions.

Without emotions, Elliot would struggle to make even the most elementary decisions. A simple question such as "coffee or tea?" could leave him stuck with an endless list of rational options. "I could go with tea, because tea is good, and so is coffee, and both are morning drinks and …" But he was incapable of "feeling" which one to choose and so he remained thirsty. A list of this kind can go on as long as your imagination allows it to, which is why you should make friends with your emotions for your chariot to drive safely in the theater of your mind as it projects into your reality.

Essence

66 *Beyond reasons are emotions, and intuition will combine them into your decisions.* **99**

Explore impulse Control

1. Today, initiate every action that involves a hand—picking up something or touching something—with your non-dominant hand. It can be as simple as writing your name, putting on socks, opening a door

2. After initiating the action, change back and continue with your dominant hand to complete the action.

3. Explore playfully.

Suspend Your Dominating Horse

1. The next decision you face, be it small or large, consider for a moment whether rational thinking or emotions are guiding your choice.

2. Consider being only rational.

3. Consider being only emotional.

4. Explore the space between them.

Train Your Intuition

1. Think intensively about a possible choice during a short time, a few minutes.

2. Do something unrelated that completely changes your state: dance, take a cold shower, kiss a frog.

3. Explore the next impulse concerning your choice. What has changed?

Dream logic makes sense, while.

~ Don T. Bidoux

TRAIN YOUR TIGER

Sometimes it doesn't matter if it's real or imagined.

~ Don T. Bidoux

You are an exceptional example of survival, hardwired to handle danger, to create automatic survival behaviors from threatening experiences, to react quickly, and to avoid them in the future. This is a security and survival system, a tiger brain of its own, functioning beyond your reasoning intellect and changing your reactions to what life puts in your path, so that life can continue doing so.

Evolution has sculpted timeless features to keep you alive, so that when you are faced with a situation that seems to threaten your safety or wellbeing, it will start by rendering you invisible. You will automatically hold your breath and freeze to gain a few seconds to search for a solution. This has fooled many a dinosaur and wolf during the voyage of your genes.

In case being invisible isn't enough, you are preprogrammed to automatically find safety, to flee, to run. Your palms will sweat to give you a grip for climbing and your heart will use adrenaline to produce more energy while your vision will create a tunnel in which you can focus on nothing but a way out.

In a defense reaction, the hands of your safety system will cover the eyes of your rational mind. There is no room for "I wonder if I can survive this challenge," when surviving this challenge requires a mind set on doing nothing but.

In some situations, there is no choice but to fight. Your tiger brain will grow you a set of teeth and claws. Should the fight seem fruitless to your experienced reptile brain, your body will resort to playing dead, hopefully confusing your predator. This is the final card of survival and it can be played with your eyes open, limbs limp, simply not responding, as in a waking dream paralysis.

One more powerful last resort that can unleash the full potential of your tiger, when nothing else prevails, is panic, a response that simply puts everything available to spin in the roulette wheel of survival.

Your tiger learns throughout life to handle challenges in new ways, and every experience adds instinctive reactions, looking to cope with future challenges.

Once a danger is over, the experience will hatch into clever pattern-spotting birds that can give an early alert from the treetops of your senses, should anything ever remind you of that situation. Sometimes they can be overly cautious, and trigger your defenses for reasons obvious only to them. These defenses are how we have survived so far, and calling them a disorder would be an insult to sixty million years of evolution.

Any form of conscious control of your breathing will regulate your oxygen balance and slow your heartbeat to where your normal thinking can come back online. You can train your tiger mentally in the theater of your mind, by rehearsing possibly dangerous scenarios and solutions to them. When the birds sing out of tune, there are a multitude of techniques to retrain them by tapping into self-regulation. Regard every action of defense as an action of defense that can be tuned and trained to respond to the realities you are facing.

Essence

"Your defense system is an amazing tiger-bird collaboration. Tune your birds and train your tiger."

Explore Your Tiger

Your tiger is activated automatically when you are caught off guard or you sense a threat. If you train for the unexpected it will be expected, and you will be better prepared to handle it. This is what doctors, military men and women, and fire fighters do. And parents should.

When your tiger is activated, parts of your brain go offline and you make way for fast, automated, survival programs such as freezing, to become invisible, fleeing if possible, fighting if you can't flee, and in worst case, playing dead (thanatosis). Knowing this can make it easier to bounce in and out of it, like most animals do.

When your tiger is activated, your security system can create a specific "flashbulb memory" of the situation so that anything in the future that reminds you of this situation will set off the alarms again. Once the trigger-response of a flashbulb memory is created, it can trigger the rest of your life even if the danger is over. This is how post-traumatic stress and phobia conditioning work. These responses can be reset.

The triggers of a flashbulb memory are a list of pieces of sensory information. They don't have to be logical or even conscious. They can be any sound, smell, taste, image, color, movement, or body position. These are your pattern-spotting birds.

The training of your tiger consists of three actions: preparing to react, regaining control, and resetting the safety switch.

There are three basic points of interaction from which you can regain control of your system during a security reaction: breathing, heartbeat, and muscle tension. These are what warriors and peacekeepers train to train their tiger. A flashbulb memory with a phobia or post-traumatic-stress can be defused permanently if you self-regulate when they are activated.

Explore Breathing

- **Relaxed breathing**: Breathe in (for a count 4), hold (for 7), and breathe out (for 8). This is 4-7-8 breathing of Dr. Weil for relaxing and lowering heartbeat.

- **Tactical breathing**: Breathe in (for a count 4), hold (for 4), breathe out (for 4), and hold (for 4). This is tactical breathing, box breathing, to regain and maintain control.

- **Personal breathing:** Find the count that works optimally for you.

Your heartbeat is key to brain and body functioning. To reach the performance you desire, adapt your breathing.

Heartbeat	Condition	Function
80	Resting	Repair, reflect and rejuvenate
115-145	Activity	Optimal performance
145-175	Extreme activity	Loss of complex motor skills
175-220	Tiger brain; Fight-flight-freeze-flop	Cognition goes offline, Only gross motor skills, Reflex behaviors, trained or not, Tunnel vision, Emptying of stomach, Normal memory offline (blackout), Traumatic memory programming active, Immune system offline, Adrenaline, cortisol and norepinephrine, Vasoconstriction to stop bleeding

Tune Your Birds

A technique that can reset the fight-flight reflex and lower stress is the Trauma Tapping Technique (TTT) as described in *Trauma Tapping Technique: A Tool for PTSD, Stress Relief, and Emotional Trauma Recovery* by Gunilla Hamne and Ulf Sandström (Peaceful Heart Network, 2021).

Think lightly about whatever bothers you and using two fingers, tap firmly and rhythmically, at a fairly fast rate, approximately 15 times on each point shown below. Take two deep breaths, relax, and repeat the whole sequence on the opposite side. Take two deep breaths and relax again when done. Repeat until calm.

NOTE: The Trauma Tapping Technique belongs to a field of psychosensory techniques designed to resolve emotional imbalances. TTT is developed on the shoulders of Thought Field Therapy (TFT) and related to Emotional Freedom Techniques (EFT) with respect to the tapping of body points. It It is designed to be content free and language-independent.

Reconsider PTSD

Consider the acronym PTSD being for a Perpetuating Traumatic Stress Defense.

The engine is not the driver.

~ Don T. Bidoux

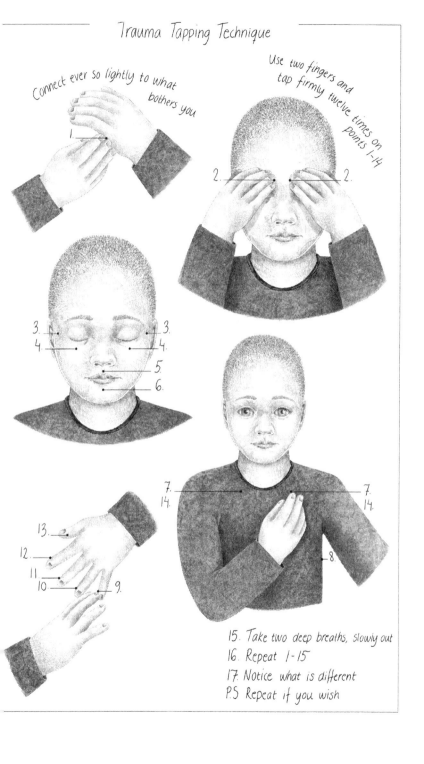

CRUISE CONTROL

Where you arrive, your habits brought you here.

~ Don T. Bidoux

There are paintings that are like disconnected color dots, and when you take a step back they transform into a beautiful and consistent work of art. There are paintings that you can look at from a distance, and the motive will evolve the closer you get.

What you think of as your personality are patterns of behaviors, repeated until somebody recognizes "you" by the way you walk, talk, react, and appear in the theater of their minds. Take a step back and put on your artist's hat. Look at the colors possible beyond those that have been used up to now.

Habits are learned in many ways. The squirrel that collects nuts for winter may do so the first time by following the example of others; it's the same for the bird that flies south. Picking the fleas from a fellow chimpanzee can fulfill the needs of protein, less itching, and connection. The habit of drinking nectar helps flowers reproduce without the bumble bee knowing it is so.

When a habit grows in the garden beyond the sun of conscious thinking, it is usually looking to fulfill something, and it can continue a lifetime interacting with the bumble bee without it knowing so. If it evolves into an unwanted side effect, the habit usually gets the blame and is forced to stop, while the need may continue unmet. Biting nails to a certain degree keeps them short and nerves in check, and after a certain point it can become a handful of pain where soothing the nerves can be more efficient than dipping the nails in vinegar, saving that for a salad.

Once you have mastered the art of walking, you can enjoy the scenery as you perform it, without thinking about it. You may not have thought about it but speaking a language and holding a conversation are learned habits, and once you do them without conscious effort, you can focus on the content.

There is a belief that habits are hard to break, and this is true if you believe it. Habits are lazy, you don't need to break a habit to change it. Just find another habit that solves the same goal. If you make it a habit to explore alternative habits you will enjoy the accumulative effect of multiple options, much like the crab that walks on both land and water and seems to think nothing of it.

Habits are best planted small and cared for until strong enough to grow on their own. If you wish to create a daily habit, start at a ridiculously low, but regular level, maybe a minute a day. Once it starts happening on its own you can easily scale it to any number of minutes. If there are things you feel a need to do regularly and cannot muster a wave of joy to surf on, make them a habit that happens while you don't even notice. If you feed a dog at the table, it will beg forever. Reward a dolphin with a sardine at the right moment and it will jump hoops without thinking twice, and so will you.

A lot of your emotional and thought patterns are habits. Worrying is a habit of looking for things that may go wrong, instead of always looking for what can go right. So is giving up if it isn't going to be perfect or settling for good enough. Say yes to people instead of no. Say no instead of yes. Snooze in the morning or jump out of bed. Look to have fun or try to win. Keep all options open or plan in detail far ahead. You created these habits, and you can change them, because they are not you; they are what you do, because at some point, you did. Becoming aware of them is the first step to conscious cruise control; refining and forgetting them is the next.

Make it a habit to take care of yourself, to find the you in the shoulds, and the time to laugh in the need-to's. Make it a habit to embrace your mistakes, and then get back in the saddle and focus on what you would like to have happen next. Make it a habit to read and to sleep. Make it a habit to love.

Essence

66 *Good habits can get you a long way without thinking about it.* **99**

Explore the Habit of Thumbs

1. Clasp your hands together.
2. Notice which thumb is on top.
3. Change all fingers so that the other thumb is on top.
4. Notice how it feels.

Micro Explorations

Expand habits: It is easier to expand an existing habit than to create a new one. What can you add to your morning routines?

Start small: Start so ridiculously small it's impossible not to succeed.

Don't break them, make them: Instead of trying to break old habits with force, create better ones resolving the same needs.

Disappear: Try disappearing a moment every day and notice what doesn't happen.

Make habits a habit: Explore what it takes to create a new habit. It's not a habit until you do it without thinking. What does it take to start?

One step ahead: Try to identify what happens just before a behavior you dislike happens, and do something different in that very moment. Anything.

Luck, like all other skills, is a habit that increases with practice.

~ Don T. Bidoux

PRIME YOUR OPTIMUS

Fate rarely calls upon us at a moment of our choosing.

~ Optimus Prime

A cat lands on its feet by design of evolution, and a circus artist can prime themselves to do the same. Progress is about finding out how to get back on your feet rather than never falling. In the face of the unknown, you will want to confront reality with questions that lead you forward and the faith to ask them.

Asking "why?" is a question that guesses the past. Asking "where to from here?" and "how?" will allow maps of what you want to have happen next to be created in your mind. They will prime you just like every thought you allow yourself to think, will create a sensation of a direction. Make sure to ask questions that paint a future you wish to look back upon, in the canvas of your mind.

Create patterns of action that can lead you forward when there is little or no information. When you are faced with a probability without answers, jump over that answer by creating two options: What if it is so? and What if it isn't so? Options prime your system for more options. The organism with most options prevails even in chaos.

Avoid getting stuck in the bystander effect by priming yourself to take a bird's eye view of a situation, and then focus on what is within your reach to change, letting go of what isn't. Look for an outcome, imagine what a next step can be and take it. Actions will keep you in the empowered front seat of your fate, and sometimes not doing anything is an action as long as it is intentional.

Every storm you survive holds the potential of helping you through emotional reactions and irrational fears in the future. Look to grow a skin of experience that will allow you to smile at the next thunderstorm, this time knowing where to look for shelter. Emotions are notions to guide your decisions, suggestions built on perceptions of what seems to be going on. Understanding how to watch them flow from the safety of the river bank rather than being swept away by them leaves you with an upper hand of options when fate deals its next round.

Most of your decisions and actions started growing a long time ago. In fact, the world is full of forces looking to prime you. Marketing primes you to desire what makes a business prosper for some, religion to respect the rules, norms and values of a specific collective. Careless comments that diminish the values of other living beings prime you to be blind to injustice as it plays out in full view. Today is a great time for starting to filter this ongoing rain of conditioning and to start thinking and acting on purpose; for planting the seeds of your future, built on values you have consciously made yours.

Prime yourself for travel, for cooking, to make a fire and to put it out, for making a stranger a friend, and for reaching out to a friend when you need to. Sometimes the diamond you carry within can only be discovered through the eyes of another person. Ask a friend to describe your best qualities from their perspective. It may allow you to discover your wings. Now, fly.

Essence

" *When an opportunity lands at your feet, be ready for it.* **"**

Prime Your Optimus

Your future actions start in your mind today. If you could prepare yourself for what you have no idea about, and it would make a big difference, what will you do differently right now?

Micro Explorations

Take care, take risks: Ignorance is no protection from mistakes. Don't let this stop you.

Just add water: What else do you need to learn about surfing before the next wave comes?

If we all did the things we are really capable of doing, we would literally astound ourselves.

~ Thomas Edison

RIDING THE PONY OF LOVE

Your task is not to seek for love, but merely to seek
and find all the barriers within yourself that you
have built against it.

~ Rumi, Persian poet and Sufi master

Beliefs can move mountains, heal the sick, and put men on the moon. Faith is a belief that can carry you through fire. Love is an act of faith and belief. Love is the interaction of souls. Love is a continuing, caring series of actions, selflessly created for the sake of itself.

There is love of life, of nature, partners, children, self, art and of shared ideals. Love is contradictory by nature. At times it can be distributed generously and sometimes in secret or with great care. An act of love is by definition without guarantees, and it is the target of its intention that transforms it into love by understanding where it came from. It can be delivered to a door that never opens and it can shine through a cloud of misunderstanding. At its best, love respects every living being involved equally and unconditionally. Love can be blind, allowing it to travel beyond a surface. It can be naive and wise. It can seem complicated. It is simple.

The flowers of love bloom through an act, an intention expressed in a language sometimes only known to the one who expresses it. Love is a gift that transforms into full power when the one for whom it is intended recognizes it and returns it in some form.

One of the many mysteries of love lies in the acceptance of one of its actions; any living being who allows an act of love to be given to it and truly enjoys it will transform the giver of the action into a lover. Love is a mighty power in deed.

A fish will love from the water, a bird from the air. The grammar can be subtle like a summer breeze, gentle like a wave caressing a shoreline, and passionate like a thunderstorm. The writing can be invisible, readable only to those with sensitive fingertips or blatantly obvious to everyone but the shoulder it has landed on. Every love has its language. Embrace every dialect for the love of the message. Love is a mirage that becomes real in the moment it acts on the stage of an existence.

Essence

❝*Love is an act in the making of it.*❞

Explore Loving

Consider something you wish to express a love for in some way. Then look for multiple ways of expressing this love and explore them.

Keep Buying Flowers...

In a hologram each part contains the whole, in a puzzle it's the other way around.

~ Don T. Bidoux

CHAIN OF TOOLS

Beliefs are the soil in which your character and your actions grow.

~ Don T. Bidoux

As you were born into this world from the safety of your mother's womb, you started to discover what seems to be true to you. What you believe to be true, due to the experiences you gather along the way.

If you were hungry and cried, a breast may have appeared with body warm nourishment. If you were cold, you might have cried again, to find the breast reappearing, pushing it gently away, communicating "not this, something else" and maybe a blanket was wrapped around you, restoring your comfort, allowing you to understand the power of crying, because the whole world seems to be at your service when you raise your voice.

With time this probably changed, and you discovered the power of cute and giggle. Of being mysteriously solemn and responding to what sounded like "peek a boo." A map of the world is constantly growing in the footsteps of your experiences, showing you how to navigate away from the unwanted into the landscapes of joy, meaning, and pleasure.

Your map of the world starts with experiences that evolve into beliefs of what is possible, and out of this grow your values that tell you what to prefer, over something else. The result is a collection of strategies and attitudes that will inspire your actions in different contexts.

In your body, every part is connected to and contributes to every other part in an amazing and complex simplicity reaching into the universe in the same way that you share your breath with the flowers that provide your oxygen in the very dance that created life on this planet. At times we seem to forget the foundation of this collaboration as we seek to explore the resources of its wonderful opportunities, beyond a climate of sustainable eternity.

The potential of paradise are seeds in your mind. All you need to do is plant and water them, and to do so in accordance with an ecology of values sprung from what is evident. No change is too small, because if you alter the course of a firework ever so slightly it will end up in a very different place. You have an impact on the ecology of this world. Explore it in the name of joy, meaning, and pleasure, making sure it does not hinder any other living being from their joy, meaning, and pleasure now or in the future. Including your future self.

Essence

66 *What life causes you to believe to be true and valuable will create the attitudes that guide your actions.* 99

Explore the Border between Believe and Know

The map of your existence will seem to be true. This is the nature of it. Is it really though? When people are asked what they know to be true, they will often answer this way:

"I know that the sun will rise tomorrow."

"I know that I am alive."

"I know that I am reading this word."

With every wish to maintain the stability of your boat, ask yourself softly, "Is it truly so, beyond any possible doubt, or is there another possible construction of a reality where it is an illusion that I have created in what I presume to be my mind?"

Now, finish this statement:

"I believe I know that _____."

"I know I believe that _____."

Explore the Values of Your Values

Every value is relative to a context and possible bene-factors. Values are the foundation of morals, and mor-als, like knowledge and beliefs, can be deceptively subjective. There is a simple way to explore them that can explain every conscious and subconscious act of free will.

1. Take what you believe to be a value. For example, "I value my health."

2. Finish this sentence: "I value my health, because _____."

3. Now, set it in relation to something you value less: "I value my health over my love for sweets, because _____ and this is why I _____."

4. Repeat from step two for as long as you find it meaningful.

Explore strategy

Every living being develops a strategy from their life experience, built on what they know, believe, and value. When you believe you have spotted a strategy in yourself, or in somebody else, ask these questions:

1. What value does it express?

2. What beliefs are necessary to develop it?

3. What life experiences can have led to these beliefs?

4. How would it read as an attitude, on a T-shirt?

We travel together, passengers on a little spaceship, dependent on its vulnerable reserves of air and soil, all committed, for our safety, to its security and peace. Preserved from annihilation only by the care, the work and the love we give our fragile craft.

~ Adlai E. Stevenson

AND AS YOU DO

Nobody is; everybody does.

~ Don T. Bidoux

Once upon a time there is you, at least you seem to be. And as you seem to be, you will always become what you currently do.

Anybody that has put together a puzzle will respect the equal value of each piece, and like a river, life seems to be a puzzle in motion, the source of which flows from survival and emotion. Should the water stop to reflect over its existence, it will no longer be a river, more like a lake, pondering itself, and if you do, make sure to ponder over that which brings the river to flow once more.

The answers to why you are happening, outnumber the stars that have lit up billions of years during the making of your being. A microbe at the start of life could have tripped and you might have been a bird instead. The value of being you, this very moment, is your pinnacle of evolution. You are art on a canvas of random events, painting yourself.

The narrative of your explorations, your ideas of the world, life, your place in it and what you may experience and contribute to it is the sun of your universe, the beliefs around which your actions will orbit. And whereas a truth may set you free, converting it into an action of any kind holds a higher guarantee of creating a change in the space-time continuum you seem to inhabit. Humankind, or just simply kind. Kindness in action.

Look around and see if you can discover what you have in common with everything, a person, an animal, a flower, a drop of water. You will find yourself everywhere, connected beyond the form and borders of what seems to be you. And since it would make little sense to bring harm to any of it, rather to enjoy it, even beyond your understanding, align your actions for the benefit of the whole, pursuing what is beyond facts, that which opens the smile of a butterfly.

If you stop for a moment, and reflect on the possibility of a meaning, you will find that it may share the qualities of a rainbow, visible at times and under specific conditions. Every action holds a multitude of possible outcomes over millions of years for billions of beings. You are a piece of this puzzle, and so is everything else. Ask yourself curiously what every moment and meeting may bring to the evolution of it all.

Essence

" Everything is connected, and you are an undeniable part of it. Let joy, meaning, and love at the cost of no other living being guide you. "

Explore the Now

See if you can forget the question "why did this happen?" and ask only,

What do I seem to have learned?

How can I use this learning in the future?

These questions are inspired by After Action Review (AAR) a structured debriefing process.

Transcend the Non-Questions

At times, you may be looking to make a decision about something you cannot know, until after. The magic spell that allows you to look beyond what you cannot know comes with two oars.

What if it isn't so?

What if it is so?

Do Not Is

If you eliminate the words *is*, *will*, and *am* from any thought or statement, you will open your consciousness to the endless possibilities of everything beyond hopeful certainty. You can use *seems* or *appears to be* instead.

"I am tired" becomes "I seem to be tired."

You can add "because ..." after and see what happens.

"I seem to be tired, because my eyelids feel heavy."

"The sun will rise tomorrow" becomes "I believe the sun will rise tomorrow, because it has so far."

Inspired by the work of Alfred Korzybski and D. David Bourland Jr. by the name of *E-Prime*.

Explore the Ripples of Your Life

1. Relax the muscles in your back and around your eyes.
2. Finish the sentence, "I am doing this because ____."
3. Finish the sentence, "And this is because _____."
4. Finish the sentence, "And this is because _____."
5. Finish the sentence "And this is because _____."
6. Can you find the first belief that led you to this action?

Sometimes you need to fry an egg

~ Don T. Bidoux

BOTTOM LINE:
THY WILL BE DONE

May the source be with you: Each body thinks, feels, and does everything for a reason. Look for it.

Your Bucket of resilience: To shift smoothly between survival, defense, and playfulness, cultivate your resilience.

Beyond reason: Beyond reasons are emotions, and intuition will combine them into your decisions.

Train your tiger: Your defense system is an amazing tiger-bird collaboration. Tune your birds and train your tiger.

Cruise control: Good habits can get you a long way without thinking about it.

Prime your Optimus: When an opportunity lands at your feet, be ready for it.

Riding the pony of love: Love is an act in the making of it.

Chain of Tools: What life causes you to believe to be true and valuable will create the attitudes that guide your actions.

And as you do: Everything is connected, and you are part of it. Let joy, meaning, and love at the cost of no other living being guide you.

THE BIG PICTURE

Dare to be holistic, dare to see the details.

~ Don T. Bidoux

As you come out on the other side of this journey, step back onto the stage of everything possible. It's a stream that never stops. How could it?

Realizing that you can create the creator of your symphony is enough already, because you have the power of good vibrations as you learn to walk like an Egyptian. You might surprise yourself as the bell tolls, allowing your Maximus to meet your Satisfix, because if you receive, thou shalt also give, and if nothing else helps, laugh.

It's actually quite simple, because your happy gene will allow your soul to survive and cooperate with your mushrooms. And as you tune your tentacles you will have a mind of your own relating to everything but you. The menu is not the meal, and we can all make beliefs from the memories of you; deciding if they should be a curse or a blessing.

Under the hood, your sovereign states will vibrate with the thrill of a skill, and you can feel it, like a baby, as you find your groove and lead your zeppelin. May the source be with you as you prime your bucket of resilience beyond reason, training your tiger into cruise control and priming your Optimus as you ride the ponies of love with a chain of tools. And as you du, remember the big picture interacting with the world, creating it as you do in the only time ever available, which will always be— right now.

QUOTING DON

"Transformation starts in exploring the doable."

"Be specific, be vague."

"When darkness embraces you, it is because it has fallen in love with your light."

"How impressive was your breakfast?"

"Thinking beings live by principles; the rest need rules."

"I got lost in reality, now I'm back in fantasy."

"True, but in a funnier way."

"In the face of life, assume not; explore."

"Where laws and norms meet morals, you find civil courage."

"Dear God, can I have some more time? I have things to do."

"Being just 5 percent more of anything can be a great thing."

"Time is precious. It's all you have."

"Sometimes it becomes fun in the head."

"Don't underestimate the freedom of a disadvantage."

"Ignorance is no protection from mistakes.
Don't let that stop you."

"It's never about you."

"Live on purpose; die with a smile."

"Bring something to the table."

"This says so much more than most people
will understand when they read it."

"Nobody is, everybody does."

"You are art on a canvas of random events, painting
yourself."

"God is created by you are created by God."

"A truth may set you free, but will it make you laugh?"

"In truth, lies trust, don't."

"Elegance is quality beyond function."

"Creating life is not the same as owning it."

"Beliefs are the soil in which your character and
actions grow."

"Never force a fart."

"What you imagine is possible."

"True beauty can wear anything, and nothing."

"Humility is the breath of wisdom."

"Think and thou shalt believe."

"Sometimes a rubber duck will do the job."

"Arrogance gives birth to ignorance."

"Every change in a living organism starts with a positive intention of some kind. This intention may not be clear to anybody, even to the organism itself."

"Luck, like all other skills, is a habit that increases with practice."

"A fundamentalist is a belief worshipper."

"Tap into the rest of the ocean."

"It's in front of us, and nobody understands it, including ourselves."

"It's not easy to find a great meme."

"This is magic, and not metaphorically."

"Fireworks are rarely impressive during the first three seconds."

"When there's no outcome, there's no limit."

"It's easier to get pregnant by mistake, than on purpose."

"Never let this quote get in the way of a better quote."

"I think you're right and it's worse."

"Understanding a joke and laughing at it are
two different things."

"Some only see what they get, not what they are taking."

"Maybe Gods are disincarnations of humans."

"Homophobia is fear of love beyond reproduction."

"The engine is not the driver."

"There's no shame in wisdom."

"You're not a snapshot, reality is a film."

"The goal of greed is imbalance."

"Sometimes, it is better, to Don your tools."

"We are the ants that can choose what anthills to build."

"You are born into an amazing machine with incredible
abilities and no manual. Do you have any idea of what you
are capable?"

"Maybe it's the same soup."

"Fun and true are not the same sex."

"To contain water, you need something other than water."

"Dream logic makes sense, while."

"There is no fun, in fundamentalism."

"Amateur is why you do something. Professional is how."

"Slowly crashing planes are very deceptive."

"Entitlement is a delusion."

"Things are not as complicated as their explanations."

"Obvious things are deceptively easy to forget."

"Everybody believes in destiny to some degree, it is fate."

"What you do affects everything. The future of this world depends on it."

"Just add water and practice, a lot of practice."

"A seed remains just so until planted."

"What is vital but not imminent can sink a ship."

"Our lack of respect for the balance of things that we don't understand is amazing."

"Entitlement opens the door of injustice."

"Maybe life is taking a break from eternity."

"Who you are is a story told by many."

"If you play the game of life to win, you are forgetting one thing."

"Everybody wants the pill; nobody wants the cure."

"Whether you do or you don't, you still do."

"Enjoy the moment, be eternal."

"The master who is no longer a student is no longer a master."

"The dreamer dreams and the actor acts."

"Where you arrive, your habits brought you here."

"Dare to be holistic, dare to see the details."

"At the end of a tunnel there is no tunnel."

"Hope is being happy now about being happy then."

"For humanity to win over nature, it must give in."

"Ignorance is no protection from mistakes. Don't let that stop you."

"Everybody wants you to do something. Make sure you are one of them."

"Why do I speak in riddles?"

"If you win over everyone, you will be surrounded by losers."

"Belief and reality create each other."

"Happiness seems to be the first and the last turtle."

"Everything, including you reading this, is a belief."

"Confusion gets you out of the box."

"Sometimes you need to fry an egg."

"Stop doing what's wrong. What's left is right."

"Some days are a lot better than others."

"In theory, life can be an illusion. In the reality of the illusion it is real."

"The rain interacts with your existence without understanding it, and so can you."

"In a hologram each part contains the whole, in a puzzle it's the other way around."

"The loveliest temptress is rarely required to explain how she does it."

"Forcing actions upon the fabric of fate is like clinging to the sun as it sets."

"No amount of shame can change the past."

"Awe can be inspired in a baby, don't complicate it."

"Where there is gratitude, there is meaning."

"Like a Danish pastry, your understanding of life affects the width more than the length."

"The truth may set you free, but will it make you laugh?"

"The thrill of a skill can be bigger than its usefulness."

"Sometimes it doesn't matter if it's real or imagined."

"Life is a cabaret in the theater of eight billion minds."

"Love is a mighty power indeed."

"Consider this sentence for a moment."

"No part of a puzzle is irrelevant."

"Look not for a reason to laugh, laugh as a reason to live."

"Your body is one of your most priceless possessions. You may wish to take care of it."

"If it feels good, it probably feels good."

"You are the main character in your movie, and a co-actor in eight billion others."

"You cannot be better or worse than anyone else. Do the best that you can be, that's all."

DON'S BOOK LIST

Books that Have Inspired All Three of Us and Our World View

The Hitchhiker's Guide to the Galaxy (Douglas Adams)

The Republic (Plato)

The User Illusion: Cutting Consciousness Down to Size (Tor Nørretranders)

The Thin Line between Cruelty and Compassion (Ludvig Igra)

The Art of Being Kind (Stefan Einhorn)

Real Magic (Dean Radin)

My Voice Will Go with You (Milton Erickson)

Man's Search for Meaning (Viktor E. Frankl)

The 4-Hour Workweek (Timothy Ferris)

Outliers (Malcolm Gladwell)

Blink (Malcolm Gladwell)

It's Never Too Late to Have a Happy Childhood (Ben Furman)

Sophie's World (Jostein Gaarder)

The Black Swan (Nassim Nicholas Taleb)

Sway (Ori Brafman, Rom Brafman)

Tales from Two Sides of the Brain (Michael S. Gazzaniga)

Conversations with Richard Bandler (Richard Bandler, Owen Fitzpatrick

The Biology of Belief (Bruce Lipton)

Make Your Life Great (Richard Bandler)

Richard Bandler's Guide to Trance-Formation (Richard Bandler)

Molecules of Emotion (Candace Pert)

The Doctor from Enköping (Stina Palmborg)

Emotional Intelligence (Daniel Goleman)

The Success Factor (Malcolm Gladwell)

You Are the Placebo (Dr. Joe Dispenza)

The Energy Cure (William Bengston)

How We Decide (Jonah Lehrer)

Teaching Excellence (Kate Benson, Richard Bandler)

When the Past Is Always Present (Ronald Ruden)

The Master and Margarita (Mikhail Bulgakov)

Resolving Yesterday (Ulf Sandström, Gunilla Hamne)

The Secrets of the Hypnotist (Fredrik Praesto)

As the Pendulum Swings (Lindsay A. Brady)

Nineteen Eighty-Four (George Orwell)

The Survivors Club (Ben Sherwood)

Crime and Punishment (Feodor Dostoevsky)

Seven Habits of Highly Effective People (Stephen R. Covey)

Blue Ocean Strategy (Kim W. Chan, Renée Mauborgne)

The Idiot (Feodor Dostoevsky)

The Trial (Franz Kafka)

The Hobbit (J. R. R. Tolkien)

The Lord of the Rings (J. R. R. Tolkien)

Tales of Mystery and Imagination (Edgar Allan Poe)

Pippi Longstocking (Astrid Lindgren)

Tao Teh King (Lao Tzu)

The Alchemist (Paulo Coelho)

The Tao of Pooh ((Benjamin Hoff)

Winnie the Pooh (A. A. Milnes)

Books that Have Made a Great Impact on One of Us

A Brief History of Everything (Ken Wilber)

Tarzan of the Apes (Edgar Rice Burroughs)

Sherlock Holmes (Sir Arthur Conan Doyle)

The Merry Adventures of Robin Hood (Howard Pyle)

20,000 Leagues under the Sea (Jules Verne)

Discworld Series (Terry Pratchett)

American Pictures (Jacob Holdt)

The Woman and the Ape (Peter Hoeg)

Zen and the Art of Motorcycle Maintenance (Robert Pirzig)

Zen in the Art of Archery (Eugen Herrigel)

The Book of the It (Georg Groddeck)

Cognitive Psychology (Smith Kosslyn)

The Body Keeps the Score (Bessel van der Kolk)

Inner Engineering (Sadhguru)

Mind Over Medicine (Lissa Rankin)

Soul-Centered Healing (Thomas Joseph Zinser)

Magick in Theory and Practice (Aleister Crowley)

A Mind of Its Own (Cordelia Fine)

The Game (Neil Strauss)

Descartes' Error (António Damásio)

The Selfish Gene (Richard Dawkins)

The Unthinkable (Amanda Ripley)

The Logic of Life (Tim Harford)

David and Goliath (Malcolm Gladwell)

Prometheus Rising (Robert Anton Wilson)

Quantum Psychology (Robert Anton WIlson)

The Inner Game of Tennis (W. Timothy Gallwey)

The Upside of Your Dark Side (Todd B. Kashdan, Robert Biswas-Diener)

The Worst Is Over (Judith Acosta, Judith Simon Prager)

The Master and His Emissary (Iain McGilchrist)

Feeding Your Demons (Tsultrim Allione)

The Origin of Consciousness in the Breakdown of the Bicameral Mind (Julian Jaynes)

Influence (Robert Cialdini)

Encyclopedia of Genuine Stage Hypnotism (Ormond McGill)

Resilience (Steven Southwick, Dennis Charney)

Neuromancer (William Gibson)

The Dancing Wu Li Masters (Gary Zukav)

Heart of Darkness (Joseph Conrad)

Hypnotic Realities (Erickson, Rossi, Rossi)

Gödel, Escher, Bach (Douglas R. Hofstadter)

One Hundred Years of Solitude (Gabriel García Márquez)

Ki in Daily Life (Koichi Tohei)

The Corpus Hermeticum (Hermes Trismegistus)

OUR INSPIRATION

Innumerable people have inspired us: relations, clients, critics, mind readers, and mentors. In the words of one, Bhaskar Vyas, MD, thank you, thank you, thank you!

Directly: Wives, moms, dads, siblings, children, friends, Tor Nørretranders, Dr. Bhaskar Vyas, Rajni Vyas, MD, Aldo Civico, Robert Dilts, Richard Bandler, John Overdurf, Connirae Andreas, Steven Gilligan, Judith Simon Prager, John Grinder, Michael Grinder, John LaValle, Doug O'Brien, Dr Ronald Ruden, Steven Ruden, Gunilla Hamne, Placide Nkubito, Jenny Eklund, James Tripp, Judy Rees, Jonathan Chase, Lars-Eric Uneståhl, Robert Sapolsky, those who agree with us, our critical challengers, and innumerable others. An extra warm thank you to Geoff Affleck for being essential in helping us over the doorstep into the physical world, and Nina Shoroplova, our fantastic editor who helps us understand the mysteries of logical grammar in contrast to hypnotic language.

Indirectly: Rumi

This may be a book without an elevator pitch,
because an elevator pitch requires a simple solution,
and maybe there isn't.

AFTERWORD

Writing this book has been an adventure that played out over more years than we imagined. We met as coaches, therapists, and mental trainers, comparing our experiences to find out why some clients change incredibly fast and others differently.

We noticed that a lot of kids and grownups with a diagnosis carried it like a hypnotic stigma. If we looked at the symptoms and reframed their usefulness, it became more of a possible superpower, like when spider man realizes he can use the spider web to jump between buildings. Up to that moment he was ashamed of it, and suddenly he's a hero instead. It's not who you are and what you are capable of; it is how, where, when and why you do it.

We started writing the Useful States Manual (USM). We looked at every symptom in the *Diagnostic and Statistical Manual of Mental Disorders* (DSM) from the point of view that a disorder is a misunderstood ability.

This led us to the importance of states of mind. How they affect everything we do. No matter how competent we may be, a poor state of mind can eclipse this competence. So, we started writing on a bigger manual: Personality Engineering, The blueprint of how we are.

This rapidly expanded into research on the brain, how many milliseconds we need to react to a thought or stimuli. How much data the brain processes, how many categories of facts our frontal cortex can keep track of at the same time (between three and seven). We looked at Adverse Childhood Experiences (the ACE study) and personality theories like the Big Five and the Disc Model. We embraced Freud, transactional analysis, and…

They all contributed to knowledge but fell short in clinical practice. When they did not provide a practical intervention for the client in front of us, they were just ideas. We needed a model that would accept and include every possible psychological model, including spirituality, Human Potential, Human Givens, the six basic human needs, the body, encoding of fear, hereditary DNA aspects, Maslow; A TOE, A Theory of Everything.

We are curious nerds and engineers. We have learned to sacrifice our darlings, and after a year of writing we decided it would not interest anybody but ourselves and those like us. So, we paused it.

We wanted to write something for everybody. We were inspired by the letters of Seneca that we read two thousand years later, and still make use of. So, we started writing in a different way. In trance. We found we had a third voice, the hypnotic voice of our combined minds in a systemic consciousness: Don T. Bidoux.

We wanted every chapter to spark thoughts, and we wanted these thoughts and emotions to be marinated in the techniques that seem to work for our clients. Simple techniques with immediate results. If it has worked for our client's, we have included it.

Halfway into the book our research took us to a website that shows how the world population increases every second. This was just before COVID-19. We both became very conscious about the earth, climate change, and how an expansion economy without a gold foot can be a slowly crashing plane for humanity. We could not write a book about personal development, without considering developing the planet. We dived into morals, values, the action pyramid, and the concept of entitlement.

When we came to the end, we contemplated adding a "Left Brain Appendix," explaining all our research and testing, our TOE model for how we humans seem to function, interact, and how we can create change by applying the principles of this model, a behavior compass that we needed to print in a 3D-printer to fully understand. Then we decided it would diminish the magic that happens when you get to explain, rather than being explained to.

Unpack Your Existence is a hypnotic dream of our work, designed to make your mind go boldly to places where your mind has not gone before, to find more of you, and bring it back for the benefit of everything.

We hope you find joy, meaning, and pleasure in it. Whatever you feel or think that you wish to communicate, please do so. We will respond in trinity.

The journey has already begun.

P.S. THESE WORDS ARE MADE FOR TALKING

There are two types of information: physical matter, such as that of the genes, and the ideas of minds. You are where they meet and evolve.

These words are designed to help you explore the many possible best versions of yourself and the world around you. If you enjoy them, pass them on.

This is what was given when you started to unpack yourself as a human:

- A physical body with a number of processes, inherent possibilities, and limitations that will direct some of your behaviors.
- An observing part of you that isn't the rational mind, the emotions, the body parts, or your reactions reading this.
- An ability to feel.
- An ability to sense what others are feeling.

- An incredible scenario simulator called imagination. Your imagination has two main tools: pattern recognition and metaphorical understanding.

- A language center that makes abstract communication and collaboration with others possible.

- A rational mind that can analyze, explain, ruminate, and plan.

- An intuitive mind that can make incredibly fast and complex evaluations and conclusions that you can't explain but just know are true, because you can feel it.

- A dreaming mind that does something else when you sleep.

- A skill set of instincts that comes prewired and has helped your species survive and thrive up until now.

- Something beyond all this that finds the beauty in art, the humor in jokes, the magic in mysteries, and meaning.

We hope the essence of this book will assist you moving through this worldly experience with dignity, wearing a smile of being curious to find out what happens next, regardless of what is next.

You can shift the future if you acknowledge it in your actions—the ecology of a truly modern human creating a paradise on purpose in balance with the rest of creation.

Your best self is a manifestation of your beliefs, values and, ultimately, what you do. Do what seem to be the right things for good reasons. Do your very best. Others will be inspired to do the same and the world will be a better place for all of us—me and you. Don't be—Do!

Don T. Bidoux, Fredrik Praesto, Ulf Sandström

P.P.S. Go back and look at any part of any chapter.

Close your eyes and notice how it resonates with what you know, and what you still may be able to learn.

In a real sense all life is interrelated. All men are caught in an inescapable network of mutuality, tied in a single garment of destiny. Whatever affects one directly, affects all indirectly. I can never be what I ought to be until you are what you ought to be, and you can never be what you ought to be until I am what I ought to be. This is the interrelated structure of reality.

~ Martin Luther King Jr.

TO-DO LIST

A global consciousness can be created,
by sharing ideas
that become actions.
Every action makes a difference,
add yours.

Made in United States
Troutdale, OR
04/18/2024

19258302R10157